Reviseand**Shine**

KS2English

Anne Loadman, Simon Greaves and Marilyn Harrop

INTRODUCTION

This book will help your child prepare for their National Test in English in a fun and interesting way. Skills and practice in spelling, writing and reading comprehension have been carefully spread over an eight-week revision period.

The book is divided into eight revision units. Each unit covers a whole week's work and for every day within that week there are two pages of content. The first page presents all the information your child needs to know in an interesting and friendly way, and the second page (the practice page), assesses their understanding of that information. **Between pages 48 and 49 there is a 16–page collection of different texts illustrating various aspects of reading and writing. These can be pulled out for ease of use when answering the activity questions.** The final part of the book contains a practice test (see page 85) which follows the format of the National English Test. Guidance is also given on how to assess your child's work and award a level (see page 92), as well as a comprehensive answer section (see page 93).

Successful revision
The key to using this book successfully is to know the ability of your child. Although the book has been designed to fit an eight-week plan, it could just as successfully be spread over a longer time. However, covering the book in a shorter time is not advised, as each child needs time to develop the depth of knowledge required.

Be guided by the ability of your child and don't be tempted to rush. If you have covered a topic and they still seem unsure, move on but come back to the other topic later. Sometimes children need time to assimilate knowledge and understanding and what seemed impossible on one day, will seem easier on another. Always try to build on success.

Talk to your child about the content of the information pages, to make sure they are clear about all the terms before they attempt the practice pages. Clear up any uncertainties by explanation or by using a dictionary. A writer's notebook is suggested by the author, as a way of developing writing; planning, drafting and redrafting take more time and space than this book can allow. The writer's notebook then becomes a helpful revision tool in itself, with examples of all kinds of writing.

Revision tips
- Regular and frequent revision is most effective.
- Aim to spend about half an hour a night on a topic.
- Don't try and cover too much at once.
- Focus on one topic at a time and go at your child's pace.
- Try not to feel frustrated if your child can't do or remember something.
- Reinforce correct answers by repeating the correct answer back to your child to show how they should be answering a particular question.
- Give hints and praise effort.

What are the National Tests?
The National Tests take place in May each year. The tests for KS2 are in English, Mathematics and Science and are administered over the course of a week. The National Test in English at KS2 is made up of three papers which are administered over four separate sessions.

The Reading Test lasts for 60 minutes which comprises of 15 minutes for reading a booklet of different text types, followed by a period of 45 minutes in which a series of comprehension questions must be answered. This activity accounts for 50 per cent of the total English Test marks, therefore it is vital that children have practice in this area before the test. The questions range from simple recall and location of information from the text, to more complex types, where the child's opinion is asked for.

The Writing Test is made up of a shorter and a longer writing task with a total of 40 marks. Handwriting is no longer assessed separately, but is assessed on the child's best writing in the writing tasks and carries a maximum three marks. It is important that children have a clear, legible, joined style well in advance of the tests.

The Spelling Test carries a possible seven marks and is administered by the teacher who reads a passage to the children while they fill in the correct spellings in their version of the passage.

The tests are marked by external examiners and the scripts are returned to the school at the beginning of July. The marks for each paper are totalled and a level is given, usually between 3 and 5. Level 4 is the average level to be achieved by an 11-year-old. It is important to note that the tests cannot be passed or failed. They measure the level at which your child is working.

CONTENTS

KS2 PRACTICE SPELLING TEST: Parent's copy

(See also page 91)

The following passage should be read aloud twice to your child. During the first reading, read it straight through. During the second reading, pause before each word shown here in bold and clearly say the word. The word may be repeated if required. There are 20 spellings in the test.

It was _____ **peaceful** _____ now. All the _____ **people** _____ had left the market and the sun had left the sky. Stalls had been _____ **covered** _____ and the market traders had gone home to count the day's takings. Philip and Rachael felt safe _____ **enough** _____ to emerge from the shadows.

_____ **Suddenly** _____ , a noise startled them. The sound of an engine roared and a _____ **bright** _____ red dustcart came to take away all the _____ **empty** _____ boxes and unsold fruit. Rachael grabbed a handful of _____ **strawberries** _____ without being seen. The dustcart roared again and _____ **disappeared** _____ over the cobbles, rattling as it passed _____ **through** _____ .

"I'm _____ **frightened** _____ !" whispered Rachael.

"We both are!" Philip agreed. "But we can't give up now. We must keep _____ **moving** _____ ."

"But where will we go, Philip? Where will we sleep?" She sucked her _____ **thumb** _____ anxiously.

"I don't _____ **know** _____ , Rachael," he said warmly to his younger sister. "But we can't stay here. Everything's _____ **changed** _____ now."

Philip did not let on how _____ **serious** _____ the situation had become. Rachael was too young to understand, but he wasn't about to let the two of them get _____ **separated** _____ . Their mother wasn't _____ **guilty** _____ of being a spy; no matter what anyone said, and they would find the evidence to prove her _____ **innocence** _____ , even if they had to walk to the ends of the _____ **earth** _____ .

SENTENCES AND PARTS OF SPEECH

What you need to know

1 How to use capital letters and full stops correctly.

2 Understand where and when to use question marks and exclamation marks.

3 Know the difference between proper nouns and common nouns.

4 Understand and use pronouns correctly.

QUESTION MARKS AND EXCLAMATION MARKS

- Questions end with a **question mark**.

  What time is it?
  Where are you going?
  How are you?

- An **exclamation mark** is used at the end of a sentence to show strong feelings.

  Stop it!
  Wonderful!
  No! It can't be true!

Don't forget

Sentences always start with a **capital letter** and end with a **full stop**.

The girl on the bike nearly fell off when she had to stop suddenly.

Please turn off the light.

PROPER NOUNS AND COMMON NOUNS

- **Proper nouns** are the names of people, places or objects, e.g. Anya, Westgate School and Tuesday.
- Proper nouns start with a capital letter.

  The capital of England is London.
  Soon afterwards Anthony came home.

- **Common nouns** are words to name people, animals, places or things, e.g. **child**, **school** and **day**.

  The book lay on the table.

Remember
Feelings, such as happiness and anger, are also nouns.

Anger is a difficult feeling to handle.

PRONOUNS

- **Pronouns** are words which take the place of nouns, e.g. them, her, it, yours.

  Josh wanted to play with the ball.
  He wanted to play with it.

  Chloe wasn't happy with Claire.
  She wasn't happy with her.

5

SENTENCES AND PARTS OF SPEECH

1 Using a red pen, punctuate the following sentences, adding capital letters, full stops, question marks and exclamation marks where they are needed.

(a) Simon: oh no i'm late

(b) Helen: where are you supposed to be Simon

(c) Simon: on my way to the football match

(d) Helen: what time does the match start

(e) Simon: kick off is at three o'clock where is my scarf Helen

(f) Helen: for goodness' sake it's in the drawer where it always is

(g) Simon: i can't find it can you help me

(h) Helen: here it is

2 Which of these nouns are proper nouns and therefore need a capital letter and which are common nouns and don't? Write the sentences out correctly underneath.

(a) I went on a cruise last year and visited: crete, cyprus, malta and majorca.

_____

(b) Of all the books in the library, my favourite is jane eyre by charlotte bronte.

_____

(c) On monday, i was surprised to see a frog at the end of my bed.

_____

(d) The supermarket in the high street is giving away balloons with every purchase.

_____

3 Rewrite the following sentences, replacing the proper nouns with pronouns.

(a) Zain was struggling with his homework.

_____

(b) Aisha had no time to play.

_____

(c) Karl's football had a hole in it. Karl would have to blow the football up again.

_____

COMMAS AND COLONS

What you need to know

1 Punctuate sentences correctly using commas for lists and to separate phrases and/or clauses.

2 Use colons to introduce a list and to join two sentences together.

COMMAS

- Use **commas** to separate items in a list except for the last item.
  Use **and** before the last item.

> In my sandwich I like egg, tomato, mayonnaise **and** cress.

- Use commas to break up complicated sentences into smaller parts to make it more understandable and to help you to make sense of it, especially if it is read aloud.

> The goalkeeper, **who was off his line**, still let in the penalty.

> **Remember**
> A *phrase* is a group of words in a sentence.
> A *clause* is part of a sentence that contains a verb (a doing word).

- A comma is also used to separate two clauses:

> I searched everywhere for my homework, but I couldn't find it.

I searched everywhere for my homework	main clause
but I couldn't find it	subordinate clause

COLONS

- Use a **colon** to introduce a list.

> Things I found under my bed: an old handkerchief, two football stickers, a small piece of bread and my little brother!

- Use a **colon** in place of a full stop if the two sentences are very closely related.

> I have news for you: you have won a competition!
> He was very surprised: he did not expect to win.

COMMAS AND COLONS

1 Use commas to punctuate these lists.

(a) Susie decided to invite Julie Carrie Jane and Sarah to her party.

(b) John prepared a meal of cold meats potatoes salad and bread.

(c) The cat leapt out of the window ran along the path then hid under the car.

(d) Ivy told me she lived at 5 Briar Road Newtown Yorkshire.

(e) The cold wet windy weather made Simon miserable.

2 Use colons to punctuate these sentences. Some introduce lists: some join sentences.

(a) Omar's school bag contained many things books, pencils, pens and sweets.

(b) The witch put in her cauldron mice, serpent's skin, school custard and tapioca.

(c) Gary gave the teacher his home address 12 Lilac Gardens, Oldwood.

(d) Anne did not realize how late it was she had lost track of the time.

(e) Ali was unsure of where to go he was lost in the maze.

3 Now use commas to separate the phrases in these sentences.

(a) Helen trying not to laugh admired her sister's new haircut.

(b) Mr. Fenwick who was making everyone a cup of tea was unaware of the argument brewing in his living room.

(c) Mina listening carefully wrote down the instructions.

(d) Scott at the back of the class had fallen off his chair.

(e) The netball player having just joined the team was very nervous.

SPEECH MARKS

What you need to know

1 Identify where speech marks should be placed in a sentence.

2 Write sentences punctuated by speech marks.

3 Understand the difference between direct and reported speech.

4 Know a range of verbs similar in meaning to the word 'said'.

WHERE TO USE SPEECH MARKS

- When you are writing conversations, every time a new person speaks, you should start a new line.

> "D'you know the capital of Alaska, Brian?" asked Stevie.
> "Yes, that's right!" replied Brian.
> "What do you mean that's right? I'm asking you a question!" said Stevie.
> "Well, Juneau is the capital of Alaska!" retorted Brian.

> **Remember**
> The rule is:
> "66, 99, new speaker, new line!"

DIRECT AND REPORTED SPEECH

- **Direct speech** means the actual words that people say. They need to be surrounded by **speech marks** which look like this: "   "

- Speech may be introduced by a comma.

> Sarah said, "Why are you crying?"
>
> The two children shouted, "Goal!"

- In **reported speech**, also called indirect speech, you do not need to use speech marks, as you are reporting back on what somebody else has said, rather than quoting them directly.

> George said that Narinder had arranged to meet him at six o'clock. Chloe told Gary that she wasn't feeling well and that he should go to the party without her.

ALTERNATIVES TO SAID

- It is much more interesting if you choose different words that describe how somebody says something, e.g. she muttered, he whispered, they shouted.

- More alternatives to said can be found by using a thesaurus or by reading books and underlining words which other authors use.

asked	called	chattered
demanded	chirped	mumbled
uttered	cried	whispered

9

SPEECH MARKS

1 Add speech marks to the following sentences.

Remember, speech marks go around the words people actually say.

(a) The guitarist complained, My string has snapped again!

(b) The crowd shouted, More! More!

(c) Who can find Australia on a map? asked the teacher.

(d) Are we nearly there yet? whinged the children in the back of the car.

(e) It was my fault, admitted the pupil, I broke the ruler.

2 Select the most suitable word or words to use instead of 'said' to reflect how these sentences were spoken. A choice of words has been provided in the box.

| whispered | cried | demanded | stuttered | shrieked |

(a) "Come closer and listen carefully," _____ the secret agent, we may be overheard.

(b) "Spot, put that down now!" _____ the dog owner.

(c) "Omkar!" _____ the excited girl, "I didn't expect to see you here!"

(d) "Wh-wh-what d-do you m-mean g-ghosts?" _____ the frightened boy.

(e) "It's so unfair!" _____ Bettina, "She gets everything!"

3 Rewrite each of these sentences as reported or indirect speech.

(a) Karl shouted, "I'm off to the match!"

_____

(b) Abbi said, "I had a lovely time in Florida!"

_____

(c) Liam replied, "My school report was really good this year!"

_____

PARAGRAPHS

What you need to know

1 Identify paragraphs in writing.

2 Understand how to organize work into paragraphs.

3 Know that paragraphs are groups of sentences about a common theme or idea.

WRITING IN PARAGRAPHS

- **Paragraphs** make stories and reports easier to follow and help to organize your work.

- When you start a new paragraph, you need to **indent** it, i.e. start writing a little bit further in from the edge of the page than normal.

> **Remember**
> A **paragraph** is a group of sentences about one topic or idea.

Peter had waited all day for the rain to stop. Torrents of water had rushed down the window pane like rivers on their restless way to the sea. Would it ever stop? he wondered.

Suddenly, as if a tap had been turned off in the sky, the rain stopped, and, where only moments before grey clouds had been, a rainbow appeared. Peter smiled. Everything was fine again.

NEW IDEA, NEW PARAGRAPH

- Every time you change the scene, or something new happens, start a new paragraph. When you are writing stories, imagine a film is being made of your story and start thinking like a film director!

PARAGRAPHS

1 Look at Text 1 in the text section: *Fair's Fair*, by Leon Garfield.
There are three paragraphs in this passage. Read the passage carefully and then write down what the main idea of each paragraph is about.

Paragraph 1 _____

Paragraph 2 _____

Paragraph 3 _____

2 Read Text 2: *Jenny Pigtails*.
Rewrite the passage, organizing the work into three sensible paragraphs.

Remember to start each new paragraph a little further in.

_____

_____

_____

_____

_____

_____

_____

_____

_____

3 On a separate piece of paper, write three paragraphs about a pop star or a sports personality that you particularly admire.

Paragraph 1: write who they are, what their achievements are and why you like them.

Paragraph 2: give a physical description of your chosen person.

Paragraph 3: write about what you would say to them if you met them.

SPELLING: DOUBLE CONSONANTS

What you need to know

1 Know the difference between a short vowel and a long vowel sound.

2 Identify double consonants in words.

3 Know and use the rule for double consonants.

SHORT AND LONG VOWELS

- Vowel sounds may be short, as in s**ta**mmer, p**e**pper and b**u**tter.

- Vowel sounds may be long, as in g**a**te, h**e**re, **i**ce, c**o**de and **u**se.
  In words with long vowel sounds like these, the vowels sound like: 'ay', 'ee', 'eye', 'oh' and 'you'.

DOUBLE CONSONANTS

- When a vowel sound is short, in a word of two syllables, it is often followed by two consonants, which are both the same letter (**double consonants**).

Double consonants	Double consonant words
bb	bubbles, abbey, rubber, rubbish, wobble, cabbage, cobbler
dd	toddler, saddle, middle, adder, ladder, paddle, address
ff	toffee, offend, differ, affect, office
gg	luggage, baggage, dagger, goggles, haggard, juggle, trigger
ll	follow, gallop, collar, yellow, ballet, village, bully, silly
mm	comma, commence, hammock, grammar, mammal, rummage, simmer
nn	penny, sunny, manners, funnel, banner, cannon
pp	apple, appear, happy, supply, oppose, happen, slipper
rr	lorry, carry, ferry, narrow, merry, mirror, errand, sparrow
ss	gossip, lesson, passage, message, issue, missile
tt	butter, lettuce, cottage, bottom, batter, kitten, cattle
zz	drizzle, puzzle, fizzle, buzzing, fuzzy, dizzy, grizzly, sizzle

Quick tip

A good way to learn your spellings is to use this strategy: Look, Cover, Write, Check. You look at the word you are trying to spell, cover it up while you try to spell it and then check to see if you have got it right. If you were wrong – try again.

Now try this!

Open a book and select a page at random. Find any words spelt with a double consonant sound. Make a list of those you find, like those in the list above, then using the Look, Cover, Write, Check method, see if you can spell them.

SPELLING: DOUBLE CONSONANTS

1 In the following sentences, underline the double consonants.

(a) The bubbles in the bottle were fizzing with great effect.

(b) The sunny meadow was humming with the sound of bees buzzing.

(c) Fluffy pillows are better than flat ones!

2 Fill in the blanks in the sentences with double consonant words.

(a) A pool of water on a road or pavement is called a p_____.

(b) I looked at my reflection in the m_____on the wall.

(c) The w_____ on the chocolate bar was colourful.

(d) The postman delivered the l_____ to the waiting child.

(e) I was m_____ my family while I was away.

3 Now the double consonant words have been mixed up to make anagrams. Unscramble the words and test yourself spelling them.

deldra _____   tubret _____   gglugea _____

denslyud _____   nolses _____

4 Here are ten words to spell, using the Look, Cover, Write, Check method.

Look then Cover	Write and Check		
	1st attempt	2nd attempt	3rd attempt
suddenly			
smuggle			
cropped			
yellow			
carrot			
hottest			
wedding			
drizzle			
affect			
swimming			

ADJECTIVES AND ADVERBS

What you need to know

1 Understand what adjectives are and be able to use them effectively.

2 Understand what adverbs are and be able to use them effectively.

3 Realize that word choice is important in all forms of writing.

ADJECTIVES

- **Adjectives** are describing words that tell us more about a **noun** (a naming word).

  The blue ball.

  The adjective in this phrase tells us what colour the ball is.

- When you use more than one adjective in a sentence, separate each one with a comma, until you get to the last one.

  High up in a tree I saw the long, colourful, tangled string of the kite.

- Adjectives can also come after the noun.

  Katie thought the boy was rude, arrogant, big-headed and loud.

ADVERBS

- **Adverbs** are describing words that tell us more about **verbs** (doing words).

  He ran quickly.

  Quickly tells us how the boy ran.

- Sometimes, a phrase is used after a verb to tell us more precisely how something is done. We call this an **adverbial phrase**. It is a collection of words that tells us more about when, where or how an action took place.

  The boy waited, more and more anxiously, for the bus to come.

  More and more anxiously is an adverbial phrase in this sentence.

- Adverbial phrases can come in different parts of a sentence, not just straight after a verb. Try swapping them around for different effects.

- The words very or quite are often added before adverbs to make adverbs more precise.

  He ran very quickly.   She felt quite ill.

- As well as quite and very, you can use other words in front of adverbs to show more precisely how a verb is being carried out: so, really, too, more, rather, extremely.

  The car drove so fast that the tyres smoked.

  The chicken, on seeing the fox, flew extremely quickly to the top of the roof.

Spice up your poetry and story writing
A really good place to find examples of adjectives and adverbs is in a **thesaurus**. Look up a simple word like nice and see how many words which are similar in meaning that you could use instead.

Quick tips

ADJECTIVES AND ADVERBS

1   Fill each space with suitable adjectives. A thesaurus might help you with your choice!

(a) The _____ centre forward placed the _____ ball on the penalty spot.

(b) The _____ baby played with its _____ , _____ rattle.

(c) The _____ crowd held its breath as the _____ runners waited at the start.

(d) In the _____ , _____ grass, the _____ watch could not be found.

(e) The _____ , _____ detective, easily solved the case.

2   What would be the best adverb or adverbs to go in each sentence?

Don't forget, you can use 'really', 'very' etc. along with your chosen adverb.

(a) The spy crept _____ and _____ up the stairs.

(b) I laughed _____ at the joke.

(c) The dog ate his food _____ .

(d) The wind blew _____ and _____ through the trees.

(e) Abbi wrote _____ and _____ in her diary.

3   Choose the best adverbial phrase to go in each sentence.

in a loud voice	as quietly as they could	more than ever
like crystal snowflakes	at the far end of the street	

(a) _____ , she wanted to win the competition.

(b) The feathers fell, _____ , from the burst pillow.

(c) _____ , the child shouted across the valley.

(d) The old clock had stood, _____ , for many years.

(e) The mice scuttled across the floor, _____ .

CHARACTERS

What you need to know

1 Understand the importance of 'well-drawn' characters in a story.

2 Be aware of how other authors introduce characters.

3 Plan a 'character sketch'.

4 Use knowledge of adjectives and adverbs to make characters more interesting.

BRINGING CHARACTERS TO LIFE

- Authors have different ways of describing **characters**.

  Re-read Text 1, an extract from *Fair's Fair*, to see how Leon Garfield **describes** the character Jackson. He tells us a lot about the character in just a few sentences.

- Sometimes **dialogue** between two characters can tell us a lot about the nature of those characters.

  Read Text 3, an extract from *The Lion, The Witch and The Wardrobe*, to see how C. S. Lewis uses dialogue to make his characters come to life.

- Sometimes how the characters behave can tell us more about them.

  Read Text 4, an extract from *Harry's Mad*, to see how Dick King-Smith tells us about Harry's **personality** just from how he comes downstairs.

PLANNING AN INTERESTING CHARACTER SKETCH

- Before you write a story, plan out a 'character sketch'. This is a brief description of your character.

  Make notes on their appearance, age and personality. You don't have to write whole sentences, just key words and perhaps your favourite phrases.
  Think about what the character is like inside and out. What motivates them? Are they brave, timid, happy or sad?

  Then when you come to describe a character in your story, you can use **adjectives** and **adverbs** that reflect exactly your character's appearance and personality.

  Maria was a slightly-built child, with shoulder-length, auburn hair that hung in loose curls. She nibbled her sandwich with quick and tiny bites, like a nervous mouse.

Quick tip

It is a good idea to collect words and phrases to do with characters in a notebook, to use when appropriate.

CHARACTERS

1 Fill in the blanks in the character description below with the best word choices from the box below.

dirty and crumpled like an old paper bag	sharp points on his face
looked a lot older than thrust into bottomless pockets	small, beady

Graham was the youngest in his family, although he _____

his 25 years. His face was _____. His

_____ eyes were nut-brown and made

_____. He rarely smiled; he had nothing to smile about.

Hands _____, he trudged through the early morning

streets towards the factory. Another hard day, he thought to himself.

2 Make a WANTED poster on a sheet of A4 paper.

First write a description of the wanted person. The character may be an escaped criminal, someone who is lost, or perhaps an old friend with whom you've lost touch. Who they are must come from your imagination. You must include: a name, a physical description and some information about their personality.

Include a drawing of your character in the box on the right hand side of the poster. Ask someone to read your character description.

WANTED

_____
_____
_____
_____
_____
_____
_____
_____
_____
_____

SETTING THE SCENE

What you need to know

1 Understand the term 'setting'.

2 Become aware of how authors use setting.

3 Be able to create atmosphere through description of setting.

ESTABLISH YOUR SETTING

- The **setting** is the **location** (or locations) where a piece of writing takes place. Stories can start with a description of the setting to set the scene for the whole story.

  Read Text 5 to see how Hans Christian Andersen uses short descriptions of the setting to show what the Little Match Girl sees.

- When you are writing a description of a setting, include what you can smell, hear, feel and perhaps taste, not just what you can see. Using your **senses** makes your writing more interesting.

- Don't have too many different locations in your story, as this can be confusing; it is better to have a couple of well-described settings.

- Read some descriptions of settings by your favourite authors and write down **some** of their ideas. Then you can use them in your own writing. But make your writing unique and use words of your own wherever possible.

CHOOSE YOUR WORDS CAREFULLY!

- Careful **word choice** is essential to describe the setting and can create real **atmosphere**. Use **adjectives** and some **adverbs** to create a picture in your reader's mind. Be precise.

  It was summer, and the sun's touch seemed to melt even the normally hard pavements. The cloudless sky was punctuated only by the vapour trails of aeroplanes, jetting excited holidaymakers to their destinations.
  Down on the ground, the happy sound of children splashing each other with cold water drifted across the garden. Bees hummed a happy tune as they buzzed from one plant to another, spoilt for choice. And I lay, warm and contented, on an old picnic blanket, smelling the cut grass, and looking at the sky.

- Use **positional vocabulary** to create a sense of place.

  Above me, I saw...   A few steps in front of me...
  Up above...

19

SETTING THE SCENE

1 Write a poem about your bedroom.

Imagine you are sitting on your bed.
What can you see, hear, touch and smell?
How do you feel?

From my bed I can:
See piles and piles of printing paper,

Hear the steady ticking of my wall clock,

Smell a sock that should have
gone in the wash yesterday,

Touch the crisp cotton
sheets beneath me,

Feel at home.

Your turn

_____

_____

_____

_____

_____

_____

_____

_____

_____

2 Imagine you are standing in a garden and you have to describe to someone
else what is around you.

The writing frame below will help you to describe your setting. Use your own
adjectives and phrases to make the picture come to life.

The air was _____ around me. A few steps in front of me

I could see _____ and above me _____ .

The _____ sound of _____

could be heard and I could feel _____ . To my right,

_____ , while to my left, _____ .

If I listened carefully, I could just hear _____ and the

_____ smell of _____ filled my nose.

It felt _____ in the garden.

You can use this framework to describe any setting. Just change a few of the
words and you will create a new picture. You will soon start thinking of
connecting words and phrases of your own.

PLANNING A STORY

What you need to know

1 Plan a story quickly and effectively.

2 Understand the elements necessary to make a story interesting.

3 Understand the terms: character, setting, plot, problem and resolution.

PLANNING YOUR STORY

- Always **plan** your story before you write it. You don't have to write much, just brief notes, which outline your characters and **what** your storyline (**plot**) will be about.

- Keep good ideas, names for characters, funny things people say, interesting words etc. in a writer's notebook and then use them when you need to write a story.

- It really helps you to become a good story-writer if you read other people's stories; especially those of established authors. Choose three or four books and read just the opening page of each to see how they start. Do the same for the ending and you will soon get some great ideas.

STORY ELEMENTS

- All stories need a good start, to get the reader interested, and an ending that ties up all the loose ends, and that is as well thought-out as the beginning. Stories may start with description, dialogue or action.

- Stories need a **setting**, or settings. These are the locations where the story takes place.

- Every story, whether short or long, needs to have at least one **character**. The character is the person or creature in the story who either describes the action or who the action in the story happens to.

- Stories can be written in the first person. This is where you write the story as if it is happening to you – you are part of the story. Stories can also be written in the third person, where the action is happening to someone else.

- Dialogue can help to move the story on and tell us more about your characters.

- Stories need a problem or some kind of tension in order to keep the reader involved and engaged in your story. Whatever the problem(s), there is usually a resolution by the end of the story, unless you are writing a **cliff-hanger** ending to leave the reader in suspense.

> **Remember**
> It helps the reader if you organize your story into paragraphs.

PLANNING A STORY

1 Write a story-start for each of the three titles below. One must start with action, one with dialogue and one with description.

Story-start: *Seashore surprise*

_____

_____

Story-start: *The mysterious present*

_____

_____

_____

Story-start: *Lost in the woods*

_____

_____

2 In your writer's notebook, continue the story for one of the three titles above. Use this story planner to write brief notes first.

Who?	Problems/Resolutions	Where?
What?		**Start/Ending**

22

SPELLING: MODIFYING 'E'

What you need to know

1 Understand the effect of adding a modifying 'e' to words.

2 Distinguish between short and long vowel sounds.

3 Spell multisyllabic and compound words that contain modifying 'e'.

THE EFFECT OF MODIFYING 'E'

- When the letter 'e' is added to the end of a monosyllabic word, it changes the middle vowel sound from a short sound to a long sound.

  fat → fate   bit → bite

- The effect of **modifying 'e'** also works when the 'e' is added in the middle of a two syllable word, e.g. platelet, spaceman, pavement, hopeful.

with a	age bathe space plate change disgrace hate
with e	scene these Peter concrete
with i	fire dive spice like hike beside divide admire slice
with o	hope alone lonely clothes hotel explode whole telephone
with u	mixture fuse picture tube cube continue capture future

Can you find any more?

- There are some exceptions to the modifying 'e' rule.
  They have 'e' on the end, but don't have a long vowel sound in the middle:

police, creche (pronounced cresh), give, were, where, love, move

Can you find any others?

SPELLING: MODIFYING 'E'

1 Add a modifying 'e' onto the end of the following to complete the words.
Then write a sentence for each word.

hop___   spit___   scar___   cur___   pet___

_____

_____

_____

_____

_____

If there is a word you do not know, look up its meaning in a dictionary.

2 In the following sentences, words with modifying 'e' have been used, but
they have been muddled up as anagrams. Sort them out and write them
correctly in the sentence.

(a) The (tenvmpae) _____ was soaking and slippy.

(b) In the distance, the sound of a (phenteole) _____ could be heard.

(c) In the (lothe) _____, without his friends, Gary felt very (enolyl) _____.

(d) My (videac) _____ to you would be to do more (sriecxee) _____.

(e) If you (inutcoen) _____ to (frusee) _____ to do your work,

   I will have no choice but to send you (mohe) _____ .

3 Here is your spelling test for words containing modifying 'e'.

Remember to Look, Cover, Write, Check.

	1st attempt	2nd attempt	3rd attempt
explode			
beside			
whole			
mistake			
explore			
incline			
parade			
accuse			
restore			
collide			

LETTER WRITING

What you need to know

1 Know that letters are written for a variety of purposes.

2 Understand that a letter may be formal or informal, depending on its purpose.

3 Plan a letter, organizing information effectively.

LETTERS FOR DIFFERENT PURPOSES

- **Letters** are written for a variety of **purposes**.

to inform	to complain
to persuade	to ask questions

- The purpose of the letter will affect the **layout**, the style and the language used. Letters may be formal or informal.

> **Remember**
> Information in a letter should be organized into paragraphs, to make the writing clear.

FORMAL LETTERS

- You would write a **formal letter** to someone you don't know, or to an organization such as a local newspaper or council. The letter would include your address, the address of the person receiving the letter and the date. You would start the letter: Dear Sir/Madam and end with Yours faithfully.

  Read Text 6a, a letter to the Langfield Echo, as an example.

Barn End,
Bridge Street,
Easton

Easton City Council,
Town Hall,
Easton

1 Dec   2003

Dear Sir/Madam,
I am writing to complain...

INFORMAL LETTERS

- An **informal letter** would be written to someone you know quite well. You would include your address and sign off, Yours sincerely or even Love from.

- At other times you might write a note to your mum, a friend, or to yourself! These notes are very informal. They don't need an address and they may not even be written in proper sentences.

Dear Mum,
Gone to Gary's.
Be back at 6.
Love Jim

Now try this!
Read the Letters page in your local newspaper. If there is a topic that you feel strongly about, why not write a letter to the paper yourself? You may get it published. Or, if you have recently received a gift, why not write a 'Thank You' letter to the person who gave it to you?

LETTER WRITING

1 Read the two letters in Texts 6a and b.

(a) Why is the writer of the first letter hoping that her letter will be published in the newspaper?

_____

_____

_____

(b) From the information in the first letter, explain how cars parking in front of the school gates are affecting the safety of pedestrians.

_____

_____

_____

(c) Why do you think the editor of the local paper wants to attract people to the public meeting?

_____

_____

_____

2 Read and compare the two letters in Texts 7a and b.

(a) Give **two** ways in which the two letters are different from each other.

(i) _____

(ii) _____

(b) How do you think Mr Nettleworth and Jonathon will feel when they receive their letters? Give reasons for your answers. Refer to parts of the text to support your answers.

_____

_____

_____

FORMAL AND INFORMAL LETTERS

What you need to know

1 Use a letter frame to help organize your writing.

2 Write a formal letter.

3 Write an informal letter.

ORGANIZING YOUR LETTER

- Plan what you want to say before starting to write.

- Jot down notes that you can rearrange to make your letter as good as possible.

- This Letter Writing Frame will help you to organize your writing, whatever kind of letter you need to write.

Remember
Information in a letter should be organized into paragraphs, to make the writing clear.

Quick tip

Formal letters should include:
- your address
- the address of the person to whom you are sending the letter.

You must write clearly, in carefully punctuated sentences.
You will need to end your letter, **Yours faithfully**.

Informal letters are written to people you know.
You could end with **Yours sincerely** but if you are writing a letter to a friend, you may finish with **Best wishes**, or even **Love from**.

Is my letter **formal** or **informal**?
Who is going to receive it?
Where do I put the address and date?
What is the tone of my letter, e.g. friendly, angry, complaining, sad, questioning?
What points do I want to make? (*Put your main points first.*)   •   •   •
What questions do I want to ask/information do I need to find out?   •   •   •
Which words and expressions would be good to use?
How will I end my letter?

FORMAL AND INFORMAL LETTERS

1 Using the Letter Writing Frame on page 27, plan a letter to a newspaper to inform or persuade people of something about which you feel strongly.

Choose one of the following topics:
- Why you need a new playground in your area
- Why the council should give you money to improve your school playground
- The need for a safe place to cross the road near your house
- Whether or not dogs should be allowed in the public park.

2 Prepare a brief letter to a friend, telling them about an event that has just happened, e.g. going on holiday, getting a new pet, receiving a present.

Think about the layout, choice of language, style and ending, using the sample letter (Text 7a) to help you with the format.

3 Why not write a letter to your favourite sports personality, film star, pop star, or other famous person, asking for some information, or just telling them how much you enjoy their work? If you are lucky, you may get a reply.

INSTRUCTIONS

What you need to know

1 Understand how to organize instructions.

2 Answer questions about a set of instructions.

ORGANIZING INSTRUCTIONS

- **Instructions** tell us what to do or how to do something. They are used for a variety of purposes.

  | in recipes | assembling a toy | how to play a game |

  directions of how to get somewhere

- When you write a set of instructions, take time to plan the order you put them in. This is really important; muddled instructions are very confusing. If materials are needed, list them first. That helps the person who is following the instructions to get everything ready before they start.

- Instructions are ordered using numbers or bullet points. They must follow a sequence, i.e. the order in which it is necessary to do things.

- Subheadings may be used to organize your instructions and make them clearer.

- Key words in instructions may be <u>underlined</u> or written in *italics* or in **bold**. Look out for these.

- There are lots of words common to nearly all instructions. Words like: first, secondly, then, after that and finally all help you to follow instructions.

- Use imperative language.

  | Cut around the lines. | Fold carefully. | Take 400g of flour. |

Quick tips

- Instructions should be short and straightforward.
- Pictures or diagrams can be very helpful.

INSTRUCTIONS

1 Number these instructions 1 to 7 in the correct order for making a cup of coffee.

- Secondly, take the kettle and fill it with water. ☐
- Finally, stir it well, sit back and enjoy it. ☐
- After filling the kettle, switch it on. ☐
- While you are waiting for the kettle to boil, put a spoonful of coffee in the cup or mug and, if you like, a spoonful or two of sugar. ☐
- Once you have poured in the water, add a little milk. ☐
- First, you need a kettle, a cup or mug, and a spoon. ☐
- When the kettle has boiled, pour water in the cup until it is almost full. ☐

2 Read the instructions in Text 8: Dancing Mothballs.

(a) Why does the writer list the materials you need at the start of the instructions?

_____

_____

(b) List **four** of the imperative words used in the numbered sections.

_____   _____

_____   _____

(c) Why does the writer use words like those you have listed in (b) for his instructions?

_____

_____

_____

3 In the 'Laboratory procedure' section of the text, the writer explains that we must be very careful when we carry out this task. Choose **one** of his instructions and explain what might happen if we do not follow his advice.

_____

_____

_____

4 What does the writer mean by the word 'dance', in the second paragraph?

_____

ANALYSING INSTRUCTIONS

What you need to know

1. Organize and sort instructions.
2. Write a set of instructions.

PLANNING INSTRUCTIONS

- Here is an Instructional Writing Planning Frame to help you write instructions.

- Think about the points you want to make before starting to write.

Remember
- List any materials that people will need at the beginning of your instructions.
- When writing instructions, use commands: *take* a spoon, *fold* a corner.
- Use subheadings to organize your instructions and make them clearer.
- When you have written instructions, read them again and think, 'If I hadn't written this myself, would I be able to understand and carry out these instructions?'

What is the purpose of my instructions? (*What do I want people to be able to do or understand from them?*)
Who are the instructions intended for: a young child, a classmate or an adult? (*This will affect the language you use.*)
Will I need to make a list of things people might need before they start to follow my instructions? (*If so, list them here.*)
Words and expressions I might use. (*Use imperative language. You are telling someone what to do and how to do it.*)
Order of instructions : 1 2 3 4 5 6 7 (*You may need more or less than seven points.*)
How will I end my instructions?

31

ANALYSING INSTRUCTIONS

1 Read Text 9: Spy Letter. Rewrite the instructions in the correct order.

The first one has been done for you.

(i) _Firstly, find the tree with the cracked trunk and stand to the North side of it._

(ii) _____

_____

(iii) _____

_____

(iv) _____

_____

(v) _____

_____

(vi) _____

_____

2 Why do you think the spy hasn't dug up the coins for himself?

Give **two** reasons for your answer.

(i) _____

(ii) _____

3 Find at least **three** words or phrases that the spy uses to persuade you that it would be worth digging up the coins.

_____   _____

_____   _____

4 Now use the Instructional Writing Planning Frame on page 31 to plan and write your own instructions for **one** of the following:
- How to get dressed
- How to play a favourite game
- How to make a sandwich
- How to cross the road safely.

SPELLING: SILENT LETTERS

What you need to know

1 Be aware of silent letters in words.

2 Be able to spell words with the most common silent letter patterns in them.

SILENT LETTERS IN WORDS

- **Silent letters** can be seen but not heard.

- They can appear anywhere in a word.

  at the beginning (as in gnome)

  in the middle (as in listen)

  or at the end (as in lamb).

WORDS CONTAINING SILENT LETTERS

- Here is a table of words containing silent letters.

b	bomb comb crumb lamb limb
c	scene scent sceptre science scissors scythe
g	design gnat gnome reign
h	school wharf which whisper whistle ghost Christmas honesty hour
k	knee knife knight knit knowledge knock
t	bristle fasten listen
w	wrap wrath wrist wrinkled wrestle whole wreck sword wring write

Can you find any more? Write them here:

Quick tip

Look up in a dictionary any words that you do not recognize and make a note of them in your writer's notebook.

SPELLING: SILENT LETTERS

1 In the following sentences, find a silent-letter word that will fit the space and make sense.

(a) This watch is tight on my _____ .

(b) I like to _____ to my favourite music when I am upset.

(c) _____ one do you like best?

(d) I would like to have been a _____ in armour.

(e) It took me more than two _____ to finish my homework!

(f) _____ is my favourite subject. I love experiments.

(g) These biscuits make lots of _____ on the carpet.

2 Complete the crossword with silent-letter words.

Across

2 Perfume

4 The noise made by blowing through pursed lips

6 A small piece of bread

Down

1 A small biting insect

2 A plan of work

3 To draw out a plan

5 An arm or a leg

3 Here is your spelling test for words containing silent letters.

Remember to: Look, Cover, Write, Check.

	1st attempt	2nd attempt	3rd attempt
whistle			
knitting			
science			
which			
ghost			
design			
wrapper			
wrestle			
school			
Christmas			

SIMILES, METAPHORS AND PERSONIFICATION

What you need to know

1 Understand the terms simile and metaphor and know the difference between them.

2 Use similes and metaphors in writing.

3 Understand the term personification.

SIMILES AND METAPHORS

- A **simile** is used to **describe** someone or something, by **comparing** it with another.

  The drum boomed like thunder.   The lamb was as white as snow.

- Similes can be used to describe colours.

  as black as ink   as red as a rose   as green as grass

- Similes are also useful to describe size.

  as tall as a mountain   as tiny as a grain of rice.

- Sometimes, similes are used to describe feelings or personal qualities.

  He was as rich as Midas.   He was feeling as mad as a raging bull.

  Her heart was as hard as stone.   His hands were like ice.

- A **metaphor** describes something by saying it is something else.

  The lake is a mirror, reflecting the face of the land.

Similes and metaphors are often used in **poetry** to describe things in an interesting way but you can use them in other kinds of writing as well.

> **Remember**
> Use similes and metaphors in your stories and report writing!

PERSONIFICATION

- **Personification** is the presentation of an object or an idea as if it were a person with human qualities and feelings. It is often used in poetry.

  The snow whispered as it fell to the ground.

- Personification is an interesting way of writing about objects or ideas, by giving them human qualities or feelings, usually in the form of verbs.

  The flowers bent and nodded their heads at the sun.

  The rain kissed my cheeks as it fell from the cloud.

35

SIMILES, METAPHORS AND PERSONIFICATION

1 Read Text 10a: 'The Cobra', a short poem by Sharon Purves.

(a) Write down the **two** metaphors used in the poem.

_____

_____

(b) Write down the **two** similes used in the poem.

_____

_____

(c) Write your own simile to describe the teeth of the cobra.

_____

2 On a separate piece of paper, try writing a poem of your own, like 'The Cobra'. It must contain **three** similes and **two** metaphors. It can be about any animal you choose.

3 Read Text 10b: an extract from a poem called 'The Mirror', by Sylvia Plath, which uses personification.

(a) The mirror is described as 'silver and exact' in the opening line of the poem. What do you think is meant by the word 'exact' in this poem?

_____

(b) Identify **two** verbs in the poem that describe the mirror in human terms.

_____   _____

(c) Describe what you think the poet means by the line, 'I am not cruel, only truthful.'

_____

_____

4 On a separate piece of paper, try writing a personification poem about an object in your house. Give the object human characteristics by using feeling verbs.

ALLITERATION, ASSONANCE AND ONOMATOPOEIA

What you need to know

1 Understand the terms alliteration, assonance and onomatopoeia.

2 Write examples of alliteration, assonance and onomatopoeia.

Week 4 Tuesday

ALLITERATION

- **Alliteration** is a way of using several words that start with the same **consonant** sound for effect.

  silly   smelly   messy socks

  Alliteration is often used in tongue twisters.

  Peter Piper picked a peck of pickled pepper.

- You can use a few connecting words in between your alliterative words to help it make sense.

  Careful cows can always keep crunching the corn.

Now try this!
Choose a letter of the alphabet (consonants are best), and make up a tongue twister based on that letter. It must be at least five words long, like this one:

Dizzy ducks dawdle dreamily downwards.

ASSONANCE

- **Assonance** is the repetition of a **vowel sound** in a series of words.

  real deal   roly-poly   spying time

  Notice that it is the **vowel sound** (phoneme) that is the same, not the spelling pattern (grapheme).

  So, **pier** and **here** are examples of assonance, as are **rough** and **cuff**, even though they are spelt quite differently. **Fine**, **spy** and **time** are also examples of assonance, even though the endings of the words are different.

ONOMATOPOEIA

- **Onomatopoeia** applies to words that sound like their meaning.

  Crash!   Buzz

Now try this!
Onomatopoeia can be fun. Try drawing a picture to go with the word 'splash!'.

ALLITERATION, ASSONANCE AND ONOMATOPOEIA

1 Read Text 11a: the poem 'The Pond'.

(a) Find **two** examples of alliteration and write them here.

(i) _____

(ii) _____

(b) What do you think 'green-backed croakers' are?

_____

(c) What does the author mean by 'silver sparkles' in line 1?

_____

2 Read Text 11b: the poem 'Monster'.

(a) Find **two** examples of assonance.

(i) _____

(ii) _____

(b) What message is the author trying to tell the reader in this poem?

_____

_____

3 Read Text 11c: the poem 'Noisy'.

There are **seven** onomatopoeic words in this poem. Find them all.

_____ _____ _____ _____

_____ _____ _____

4 Choose a good onomatopoeic word to fill the blank in each of the following sentences.

swishing	buzzing	zoomed	splash	snap

(a) My brother loves to _____ in puddles.

(b) The angry bee made a harsh _____ sound.

(c) The rope swing was too heavy and the branch went _____!

(d) The racing car _____ round the track at 120 mph.

(e) The horse was _____ its tail at the flies.

EXPLORING DIFFERENT FORMS OF POETRY (1)

What you need to know

1 Recognize that poetry comes in many forms.

2 Know that not all poetry has to rhyme.

3 Be aware that some poetry, e.g. Haiku, has a strict form to follow.

TYPES OF POETRY

Poems do not always need to be long.

- A **Tanka** has a set number of lines and syllables. It is made up of a first line of 5 syllables, followed by lines of 7, 5, 7 and 7 syllables.

Old iron railings,
Standing like tired, old soldiers.
Rusty and crooked,
One too many battles fought;
But never leaving their post.

- Sometimes poems are written in the shape of the subject they are about. **Shape poems** give a visual effect as well as the effect of the words.

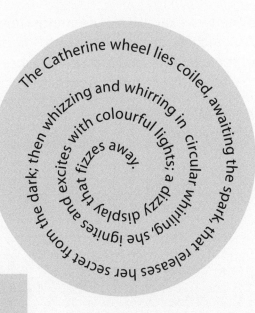

The Catherine wheel lies coiled, awaiting the spark that releases her secret from the dark; then whizzing and whirring in circular whirling, she ignites and excites with colourful lights; a dizzy display that fizzes away.

- A **Kenning** is a kind of riddle in poetry form. It describes something in pairs of words, without actually mentioning the object's name!

An itchy biter
A giant leaper
A black dot
A sore spot
A dog scratcher
A wingless wonder.
A flea.

Improving your poetry
Have your poems got the right number of lines and syllables?

HAIKU POETRY

- **Haiku**, which is a Japanese form of **poetry**, has only 3 lines with 5 **syllables** in the first line, 7 in the second and 5 in the third. The words must be carefully chosen to paint a picture in the reader's mind.

The wind blows softly,
Brushing my face with its wings,
Cooing and tender.

EXPLORING DIFFERENT FORMS OF POETRY (1)

1 Read the two examples of Haiku: 'The wind blows softly' on page 39 and Text 12a 'Snowman in a field'.
Now try writing a Haiku of your own. Think of an everyday object and describe it in your own special way.

Plan your Haiku in rough first. Count out the syllables in each line and make sure you follow the pattern of 5,7,5. Keep changing the words of your poem until you are happy with the way it reads.

2 Read the two examples of Kennings: Text 12b 'View of a Rabbit', by Mark Richard and 'An itchy biter' on page 39.
Using the examples to help you , choose your favourite animal and try to write a Kenning about it.

3 Read the two examples of Tanka: Text 12c 'Tanka Tanka' by John McIlwain, and the example 'Old iron railings' on page 39.
In your writer's notebook, try writing a Tanka about a building or car, or you may prefer to try writing a Tanka about an emotion, such as feeling angry or upset.

EXPLORING DIFFERENT FORMS OF POETRY (2)

What you need to know

1 Recognize that poetry comes in many forms.

2 Know that not all poetry has to rhyme.

3 Know what is meant by narrative poetry.

4 Know that some poetry is humorous.

NARRATIVE POETRY

- **Narrative poetry** tends to be quite long and tells a story in **verse**. This type of poetry tends to **rhyme**.

The Pied Piper of Hamelin

Into the street the Piper stept,
Smiling first a little smile,
As if he knew what magic slept
In his quiet pipe the while;
Then, like a musical adept,
To blow the pipe his lips he wrinkled,
And green and blue his sharp eyes twinkled,
Like a candle-flame where salt is sprinkled;
And ere three shrill notes the pipe uttered,
You heard as if an army muttered;
And the muttering grew to a grumbling;
And the grumbling grew to a mighty rumbling;

And out of the houses the rats came tumbling.
Great rats, small rats, grey rats, tawny rats,
Grave old plodders, gay young friskers,
Fathers, mother, uncles, cousins,
Cocking tails and pricking whiskers,
Families by tens and dozens,
Brothers, sisters, husbands, wives –
Followed the Piper for their lives.
From street to street he piped advancing,
And step for step they followed dancing,
Until they came to the river Weser,
Wherein all plunged and perished!

Robert Browning
from *The Oxford Book of Children's Verse*, Iona and Peter Opie

HUMOROUS POETRY

- In some **humorous poetry**, the writer invents their own vocabulary to describe things. This kind of poetry is called **nonsense poetry**.

In a smollet, way up high,
There lived a diggle with a huge green eye.
He dined on frams and salads of yams
And his job was painting the sky.

There is no such thing as a 'diggle' or a 'smollet' and have you ever tasted a 'fram'? They exist only in the imagination of the poet.

To find more examples of humorous poetry, read poems by Edward Lear and Spike Milligan.

EXPLORING DIFFERENT FORMS OF POETRY (2)

1 Read Text 13a: the poem 'I went to the pictures tomorrow'.

(a) In the poem where did the person sit?

_____

(b) Why is it impossible to fall from the pit to the gallery in a theatre or cinema?

_____

(c) Find **one** other impossible thing that happened in the poem?

_____

2 Read Text 13b: 'On the Ning Nang Ning Nang Nong!' by Spike Milligan.

(a) In the poem find **two** examples of alliteration.

(i) _____

(ii) _____

(b) Find **one** example of onomatopoeia in the poem.

_____

(c) Write **two** examples of 'nonsense' from this poem.

(i) _____

(ii) _____

3 Read Text 13c: the narrative poem, 'The Listeners', by Walter de la Mare.

(a) Where do you think the Traveller has arrived?

_____

(b) Who do you think the Listeners are?

_____

(c) Find **one** word or phrase from the poem that tells you what time of day the poem takes place.

_____

(d) Why had the Traveller come to the building?

_____

SPELLING: SOFT C AND G

What you need to know

1 Be able to spell words containing 'softened' **c** and **g**.

2 Know the rule for which vowels will soften **c** and **g**, and which will not.

'SOFTENED' C AND G

- Often, the letter **c** is a 'hard' 'c' sound, as in the word **cat**, but certain letters have a softening effect on **c** to make it sound like the letter **s**, e.g. pencil. Similarly, the letter **g** is often 'hard', as in the word **gate**, but certain letters have a softening effect on the letter **g**, making it sound like the letter **j**, e.g. **giant**.

Can you work out which vowels have a softening effect on each letter in these words?

Soft c words

cent	receive	receipt	palace	police	mice
circus	circle	recipe	cycle	fancy	cygnet	ceiling

Can you find any more? Write them here:

Soft g words

gentle	gesture	generous	message	giant
gymnast	gymnastic	gypsy	genuine	genius

Can you find any more? Write them here:

Exceptions

As always with English, there are exceptions to the rule: **girl**, **gill** and **gilt** all have hard 'g' sounds. Can you think of any more exceptions to the rule?

Now try this!
Choose three words from each set and write them in a sentence to show that you know what they mean. Use a dictionary to look up the meaning of any words that you are unsure of.

Remember
When **c** comes before **e**, **i** or **y**, the sound is softened.
When **g** comes before **e**, **i** or **y**, the sound is softened.

43

SPELLING: SOFT C AND G

1 Here are some words containing the letter **c**. Circle the words which have a soft 'c' sound.

cat   container   cymbal   custard   sentence   catch

creep   cylinder   crust   ceiling   dancing   climb

2 Now circle words that contain a soft 'g' sound.

gentle   ghost   gripping   gymnast   girl   gull

giant   rage   grey   germ   glue

3 Fill in each blank in the poem below with a softened **g** word.
Choose from the following words.

gigantic   giant   gymnast   graceful   genius

A _____ _____ from Slough

Made a _____ leap over a cow

This _____ athlete

Was so light on his feet

That the crowd gave a _____ WOW!

4 Here is your spelling test for words containing softened **c** and **g**.

Remember: Look, Cover, Write, Check.

	1st attempt	2nd attempt	3rd attempt
generous			
ceiling			
pencil			
garage			
cygnet			
gymnastics			
dancing			
genuine			
deceive			
arrange			

ANALYSING PLAYSCRIPTS

What you need to know

1 Know and recall the features of a playscript.

2 Understand the terms: character, action, stage directions.

3 Understand how a play is written and set out.

FEATURES OF A PLAYSCRIPT

- A **playscript** contains all the words that the actors need to say in order to perform a play.

- A play is divided up into acts and scenes.
An **act** is a long section of a play and may contain many scenes.
A **scene** is a short part of a play, a bit like a chapter in a book.

- At the start of a play, there is usually a list of all the **characters**. This tells you how many actors are needed and what kind of characters they will be.

- Every time a character needs to speak, their name is written on the left hand side of the script, in front of the words that they are about to say. This helps the actors to follow the script and learn their parts.

> **Morven:** It's getting really late. Do you think we should head back?
>
> **Steven:** No, don't be silly – we've got at least an hour of daylight left.

STAGE DIRECTIONS

- A playscript also contains **stage directions** (often in brackets), which tell the actors when they have to enter and leave the stage, any **actions** they need to do and how they need to say their words (e.g. angrily, impatiently, excitedly).

> **Morven:** (*looking at her watch anxiously*) It's getting really late. Do you think we should head back? (*turns to Steven*)
>
> **Steven:** (*smiling at Morven*) No, don't be silly (*looks at the sun*). We've got at least an hour of daylight left.

- At the start of each scene, stage directions show where the scene is taking place (e.g. in a wood, in a cave) so that appropriate scenery, **special effects** and equipment (called **props**) can be made.

ANALYSING PLAYSCRIPTS

1 Read Text 14a: *Isis and Osiris*, a play written by Ann Wade.

(a) The narrator speaks before the play begins. What effect do these words have?

_____

_____

(b) Write **two** suggestions made by Set's friends for destroying Osiris.

(i) _____

(ii) _____

(c) Explain the meaning of the word 'immortal'.

_____

(d) What is the only way for Set to become ruler of Egypt?

_____

2 Read Text 14b: *Morgan's Field*, a play written by Berlie Doherty.

(a) What kind of person do you think Cai is? Support your answer with examples from the text.

_____

_____

(b) Why do you think the author uses the phrase 'misty hills' to describe the place they have come from?

_____

_____

(c) Young Morgan lists five good points about the place they have arrived at. Choose **two** and write them down.

(i) _____

(ii) _____

WRITING PLAYSCRIPTS

What you need to know

1 Understand the term playwright.

2 Write a short playscript.

PLAYWRIGHTS

- A **playwright** is the name given to a person who writes the script for a play. The most famous English playwright is probably William Shakespeare and you will study some of his plays in your Literacy lessons.

- A playwright must decide on the names of the **characters**, consider what their personalities are like and show this in the way that the characters act and speak.

- The playwright must give **stage directions** explaining where the play is set, at what times the **action** moves to a different location, and whether the actors will need to use any **props**.

PLANNING A PLAYSCRIPT

Here is a planning sheet to help you organize your ideas when you are writing a play of your own.

> **Remember**
> When you are writing plays, every time a different character speaks, you need to begin a new line and write the character's name.
> Stage directions (in brackets) should be given where appropriate.

Play Planning Sheet

My play is called:	
It is about:	
The main characters are:	
It will be set in:	
The play will start like this:	
The main event will be:	
The play will end like this:	
The main props/scenery I will need are:	

WRITING PLAYSCRIPTS

1 Here is a conversation between four characters. Write it out again in the form of a playscript and add your own stage directions.

Morven was excited about her forthcoming holiday.
"Have we got everything we need, Steven? What about the first aid kit?"
"Don't worry," Steven replied, "I've checked everything twice."
"Have you got your passports?" asked Mum worriedly, "because you won't get very far without those!"
Just then Dad came in the front door. "Isn't anyone coming? I've had the engine running for five minutes. Don't you want to catch that plane?" he said gruffly.
Morven rushed around collecting her bags. "Come on," she said, "Let's go!"

2 Read Text 14a: *Isis and Osiris* again.
On a separate piece of paper continue the scene by writing dialogue for the three characters.

Think about how the plot will develop: the characters are trying to think of a way to get rid of Osiris. Set out the dialogue in the same style as the text.

3 Draw up a short cast list and dramatize a situation you have experienced in school.

Text 1 Fair's Fair by Leon Garfield

Jackson was thin, small and ugly, and stank like a drain. He got his living by running errands, holding horses, and doing a bit of scrubbing on the side. And when he had nothing better to do he always sat on the same doorstep at the back of Paddy's Goose, which was at the worst end of the worst street in the worst part of the town.

He was called Jackson, because his father might have been a sailor, Jack being a fond name for a sailor in the streets round Paddy's Goose; but nobody knew for sure. He had no mother, either, so there was none who would have missed him if he had fallen down a hole in the road. And nobody did miss him when he vanished one day and was never seen or heard of again.

It happened when Christmas was coming on – about a week before. Dreadful weather, as hard and bitter as a quarrel. Dreadful weather, with snow flakes fighting in the wind and milk freezing in the pail.

Text 2 Jenny Pigtails

Jenny Pigtails they called her, because of her long, red plaits. "Jenny Pigtails!" they would shout, and run away, laughing. But Jenny wasn't bothered by their names. She had more important things to worry about, and anyway, she liked her red, unruly hair. Plaiting it was the only way to keep it in check; otherwise it fell round her shoulders like a huge cape. The school bell sounded and Jenny lined up with the others. She stood behind her friend, Emily Souter, and they chatted about nothing much until the teacher came out to the line. Jenny liked Mrs. Walton, who always smiled at her and helped her to do her work. When it was their turn, Class 5 marched in. Inside, Jenny could smell antiseptic, and in a small room off the hall, she caught sight of the school nurse. Oh, no, today was the day for Class 5's TB injections and Jenny was terrified of needles!

Text 3 The Lion, The Witch and The Wardrobe by C. S. Lewis

"But what *are* you?" said the Queen again. "Are you a great overgrown dwarf that has cut off its beard?"

"No, your Majesty," said Edmund, "I never had a beard, I'm a boy."

"A boy!" said she. "Do you mean you are a Son of Adam?"

Edmund stood still, saying nothing. He was too confused by this time to understand what the question meant.

"I see you are an idiot, whatever else you may be," said the Queen. "Answer me, once and for all, or I shall lose my patience. Are you human?"

"Yes, your Majesty," said Edmund.

"And how, pray, did you come to enter my dominions?"

"Please, your Majesty, I came in through a wardrobe."

"A wardrobe? What do you mean?"

"I – I opened a door and just found myself here, your Majesty," said Edmund.

"Ha!" said the Queen, speaking more to herself than to him. "A door. A door from the world of men! I have heard of such things. This may wreck all. But he is only one, and he is easily dealt with." As she spoke these words she rose from her seat and looked Edmund full in the face, her eyes flaming; at the same moment she raised her wand. Edmund felt sure that she was going to do something dreadful but he seemed unable to move. Then, just as he gave himself up for lost, she appeared to change her mind.

"My poor child," she said in quite a different voice, "how cold you look! Come and sit with me here on the sledge and I will put my mantle round you and we will talk."

Pages 1-16 can be pulled out to make the text extracts easier to refer to when answering the questions in the revision and practice test sections.

Text 4   Harry's Mad by Dick King-Smith

Most people walk down stairs, putting one foot more or less carefully in front of the other, and perhaps holding on to the banisters. Not Harry Holdsworth, oh no, not he!

Long hours of practice had made Harry expert in unusual methods of getting from the upper to the ground floor of the Holdsworths' house.

Some were comparatively simple – sliding down the banisters for example, or rolling down the stairs, or hopping down them, feet together, one step at a time. Hopping down but missing out every other step was a good deal more difficult, and could be made harder still by doing it with hands in pockets, or even – the real test – with hands in pockets and eyes shut.

Harry only attempted this last combination when something told him it was going to be a very special sort of day.

Text 5   The Little Match Girl by Hans Christian Andersen

It was snowing and the wind grew cold as darkness fell over the city. It was New Year's Eve. In the gathering gloom a little girl with bare feet padded through the streets. She had been wearing her mother's slippers when she left home, but they were far too big, and she had lost them while hurrying across a busy road. One of them was nowhere to be found, and a boy ran off with the other. So now her bare feet were mottled blue and red with the bitter cold.

In her old apron the little girl carried bundles of matches, which her father had sent her out to sell, but all day long nobody had bought a single match from her. Cold and hungry, she made her weary way through the city. Brilliant lights streamed from the windows of big houses, where blazing fires crackled merrily in the hearth, and the smell of roast goose hung on the air, for it was New Year's Eve.

The little girl crouched down in a corner between two houses. She drew her knees up to her chest, but this seemed to make her even colder. She was afraid to go home, for she had sold nothing the whole day! Not a penny had she earned, and her father would surely be angry with her. But it was just as cold at home, for the wind whistled through the cracks in the walls and floorboards.

How wonderful it would be to light a match! All she had to do was take one out of the bundle, strike it on the wall, and warm her fingers at the flame. She drew out a match and struck it. How it sparkled and gleamed! How the flames leapt and the flames danced! It seemed to the little girl as if she were sitting at an enormous iron stove with brass ornaments on it. She stretched out her frozen feet to warm them – and the flame went out. Gone was the wonderful stove, and there she sat in the snow with the burnt-out match smoking between her fingers.

Text 6a

18, Robin Court
Langfield
Herts.

The Editor,
Langfield Echo

30.10.03

Dear Sir,
I am writing about the ever-present danger to young schoolchildren of parked cars outside my children's school. In spite of the zigzag lines, cars still park as close to the school gates as possible, obscuring the view of pedestrians and blocking the road. This means that when I pick up my children from school (on foot, of course!) I am unable to fit my pram through the tiny gap they leave open to me.
There have been hundreds of accidents near the school, and it is only a matter of time before someone is killed. All these drivers are mad and should be locked up! All the parents agree with me. Let's walk to school and save our children!
Yours faithfully,
Mrs. U. Barrass

Text 6b

Dear Readers,

Our campaign to stamp out illegal parking outside our city's schools has been gathering momentum. Thanks to you, our loyal readers, the council decided at their meeting last night to send round a police car, each morning, to the schools with the most severe traffic problems.

In addition to this, sets of posters with safety messages are available, free, from our reception desk in the High Street. If you can display one in your window, it will further help our campaign.

There will be a public meeting on Wednesday, 11th of November, in the lecture room at the main police station, Burgess Road, starting at 7 pm. This will be your chance to make your views known to the police, local councillors, the road safety department and your local MP. Of course, representatives from the Langfield Echo will also be there. Together, we are making a difference.

The Editor

Text 7a

6, Orchard Lane,
Puddlesford,
Westfield
6.9.03

Dear Jonathon,
I just had to write and tell you about my new pet. It's a dog, exactly the kind you know I wanted: a Japanese Akita. It's absolutely huge, with a dark face and enormous paws. I can't wait to get home from school to play with him and teach him new tricks. He is absolutely beautiful; you would love him.
You will get to see my new dog when you come to stay in October, because Mum has already said that I can have a friend to stay at half term. We can take him out near the lakes; he loves the water!
Oh, by the way, we call him Sam. Anyway, must go, the dog needs feeding!

Love,
Jack

Text 7b

18 Orchard lane,
Puddlesford,
Westfield

Mr T. Nettleworth
Environmental Health Dept.
Town Hall
Westfield   9.9.03

Dear Mr Nettleworth,
I am writing to complain about the number of dogs left to wander around the banks of our town lake. I was there the other night with my young daughter, when a large dog appeared from nowhere and completely knocked her over! She was shocked but, luckily, not badly hurt.
There is a sign by the lake, which states that dogs are not allowed off the leash at the water's edge, but dog-owners are clearly ignoring this. I urge you to come and take a look at the situation yourself.
Yours sincerely,

M. Thompson

It is most important to follow instructions carefully and to take basic safety precautions, especially when conducting experiments. This experiment is about "dancing" mothballs.

Dancing Mothballs

Mothballs are quite heavy and would sink in most liquids. But in this fizzy combination of acidic and alkaline substances they will "dance" in an amusing way.

Materials

- 5 or 6 small mothballs
- spirit-based felt-tipped pens
- large, glass jar and water
- 10 tablespoons wine vinegar
- 2 teaspoons sodium bicarbonate
- wooden spoon

1. Colour the mothballs with the felt-tipped pens.
2. Add water to the jar until it is three-quarters full.
3. Add the sodium bicarbonate and stir until it dissolves.
4. Add the vinegar and stir.
5. Drop the mothballs into the jar.

At first the mothballs will sink. Then they will dance upward. This happens because the acidic vinegar and alkaline sodium bicarbonate react to make carbon dioxide gas. Bubbles of this gas collect on the mothballs. The gas, being lighter than water, lifts the mothballs to the surface. There the gas escapes, so the mothballs sink again, and the chemical reaction is repeated.

Laboratory procedure

1. Put on old clothes, an overall or an apron before starting.
2. Read through an experiment, then collect the materials listed.
3. Clear a work area and cover it with newspaper or other paper. Put an old wooden chopping board or cork tile on the work area if you have to cut anything.
4. Take care not to get anything in or near your eyes. If this happens, immediately rinse your eyes in clean water, and tell an adult.
5. Never eat or drink anything unless told you may do so in an experiment.
6. Clean up any mess you make.
7. Wash your hands if you have touched a chemical, and when you have finished an experiment.

Text 9 Spy Letter

To whom it may concern,

I do not have much time left, so I am scribbling down this note. Whoever finds this, read it well; it could make you very rich! Don't ask me how I came by them, but I have buried an enormous amount of very valuable Roman coins, not far from the spot where you find this letter. Follow my instructions carefully and you will be wealthy beyond your wildest dreams! Of course I haven't made it that easy – I've jumbled up the instructions; but once you've unscrambled them, all will become clear to you!

Here is what you must do:
– Once you have spotted the branch, walk six paces in the direction it is pointing and stop.
– Finally, make sure no-one is looking and dig! The treasure is buried 30 cm below ground level and is wrapped in a plastic bag.
– The third thing you must do is make a quarter turn to the left and walk ten paces; you should stop just in front of an oddly-shaped and very heavy rock.
– Secondly, walk three large steps in a westerly direction and stop.
– Firstly, find the tree with the cracked trunk and stand to the North side of it.
– After coming to the rock, look up; you should see an overhanging branch, which will point in the direction you now should go.

When you have found your treasure, be sure not to open the bag where you stand; you may have been followed! Take the bag immediately to the police and show them this letter. Ask them to get in touch with Professor John F. Partington of the Ancient History Museum and he will come and look at the coins. You will not believe how much they are worth!
You may be asking yourself why I have not claimed the coins for myself – well that's another story. Let's just say that my duties for the government have led me on an unexpected mission and that is why I am relying on you to collect them for me. I assure you, you will be well rewarded, as the Ancient History Museum has been looking for these coins for the last ten years, since their mysterious disappearance.

Don't let me down. Don't let these coins fall into the wrong hands.
Good luck!
End of message.

Text 10a

The Cobra

His marks are honeycomb,
His eyes are like flying saucers,
His ribs stretch like elastic bands.
The curled teeth shining and ready
for a victim.
His back patterns are stars in the moonlight.

Sharon Purves

Text 10b Extract from 'The Mirror'

The Mirror

I am silver and exact. I have no
preconceptions.
Whatever I see I swallow
immediately
Just as it is, unmisted by love
or dislike.
I am not cruel, only truthful –

Sylvia Plath

From Collection of Poems by Sylvia Plath,
Faber & Faber Ltd.

Text 11a

The Pond

Silver sparkles gleam and shine,
Reflections of the summertime.
Green-backed croakers sit and stare,
As frilly fish dart here and there.
Tiny tadpoles twist and turn,
Then hide behind a water fern.
While up above in shrubs and sky,
The butterflies go floating by.

Text 11b

Monster!

Hairy, scary,
Please be wary,
Monsters can be
quite contrary.
Highly wily,
Acting slyly,
Don't believe them
When they're smiley.

Better by far to follow a hunch
Than end up as a monster's lunch!

Text 11c

Noisy!

Bang goes the door, as out I go,
Clatter down the steps to the street below.
In my boots, it feels so good,
To squelch about in slimy mud.
I splash about in puddles deep,
And crack dry branches with my feet.
I rustle through piles of autumn leaves,
And crunch through pebbles on the beach.
Then when I've run out of things to do,
I run back home and make noise there too!

Text 12a

Haiku

Snowman in a field
Listening to the raindrops
Wishing him farewell.

Roger McGough

Text 12b

View of A Rabbit

A fur lump
A secret listener
A hole digger
A swift hopper
A currant dropper
A lettuce diner
A carrot nibbler
A slight squeak.

Mark Richard

Text 12c

Tanka Tanka

Refinery of
A million thoughts and words
Into five small lines,
Each an exact number of
Syllables. Super tanka!

John McIlwain

Text 13a

I went to the pictures tomorrow

I went to the pictures tomorrow,
I took a front seat at the back,
I fell from the pit to the gallery
And broke a front bone in my back.

Anon

A lady she gave me some chocolate,
I ate it and gave her it back.
I phoned for a taxi and walked it,
That's why I never came back.

Text 13b

On the Ning Nang Ning Nang Nong!

On the Ning Nang Nong
Where the cows go Bong!
And the monkeys all say Boo!
There's a Nong Nang Ning
Where the trees go Ping!
And the teapots Jibber Jabber Joo.
On the Nong Ning Nang
All the mice go Clang!
And you just can't catch'em when they do!

So it's Ning Nang Nong!
Cows go Bong!
Nong Nang Ning!
Trees go ping!
Nong Ning Nang!
The mice go Clang!

What a noisy place to belong,
In the Ning Nang Ning Nang Nong!

Spike Milligan

Text 13c The Listeners by Walter de la Mare

'Is there anybody there?' said the Traveller,
Knocking on the moonlit door;
And his horse in the silence champed the grasses
Of the forest's ferny floor;
And a bird flew up out of the turret,
Above the Traveller's head:
And he smote upon the door again a second time;
'Is there anybody there?' he said.
But no-one descended to the Traveller;
No head from the leaf-fringed sill
Leaned over and looked into his grey eyes,
Where he looked perplexed and still.
But only a host of phantom listeners
That dwelt in the lone house then
Stood listening in the quiet of the moonlight
To that voice from the world of men:
Stood thronging the faint moonbeams on the dark stair,

That goes down to an empty hall,
Hearkening in an air stirred and shaken
By the lonely Traveller's call.
And he felt in their heart their strangeness,
Their stillness answering his cry,
While his horse moved, cropping the dark turf,
'Neath the starred and leafy sky;
For he suddenly smote on
the door, even
Louder, and lifted his head:-
'Tell them I came, and
no one answered,
That I kept my word,'
he said.

From 'The Listeners' by Walter de la Mare

Text 14a Isis and Osiris by Ann Wade

A play in eight scenes, *Isis and Osiris* is based on an ancient Egyptian myth.

Characters:
Narrator
Isis (Queen of Egypt)
Osiris (King of Egypt)
Set (Osiris' brother)
Setna (friend of Set)
Thoth (friend of Set)
Horus (Isis' and Osiris' son)
Queen of Astarte of Byblos

Scene One

The garden of King Osiris' palace

Narrator: Egypt is at last at peace. The people have learned from their God-King Osiris how to use the rich silt of the River Nile to grow crops. There is plenty to eat, fighting has ceased and the people are growing rich. Everyone is content. Everyone that is except Set, Osiris' brother. He is filled with envy for his brother. All he wants is to kill him and seize power for himself.

Enter Set, followed by his friends Setna and Thoth.

Set: I cannot bear to see my brother and his wife so happy. Soon I will be even further from power when their child is born.

Thoth: Why don't you kill him? We could ambush him one night as he walks alone in his garden.

Set: No, it will not be so easy to destroy my brother. Remember he's immortal, so we will need to be very clever.

Setna: Can't he 'accidentally' fall into the River Nile? If we make sure that we put lead weights in the hem of his robes then he will sink to the bed of the Nile quickly. No-one will be able to lift him to safety until it is too late.

Set: It's a good plan and were my brother not a god it would work. No, the only way we can succeed is for Osiris to willingly give up his life.

Silently the men walk together, deep in thought. The cutting of stone is heard offstage.

Text 14b Morgan's Field by Berlie Doherty

Scene Three

Young Morgan:	Father! Wait!
Elen:	Yes, Cai, we must rest here. I can't go any further. And besides, our people are miles behind us. Look where they are still, struggling down from the misty hills. I think we should wait here for them.
Cai:	There's no time to wait. No time to stop, I tell you. My time is short enough.
Olwen:	It would be good to rest here. It's so sheltered.
Cai:	My time is short enough. I dare not rest until I have found the right place for us to live in.
Elen:	But we've been walking now for weeks. Is there to be no rest for us, ever?
Young Morgan:	Father! Why don't we stop here?
Cai:	I've told you…
Young Morgan:	Not to rest, Father! To live!
Cai:	To live! Here! You think this is where our journey ends? Look at it.
Young Morgan:	This has to be the place we're searching for. Mountains – fold on fold of mountains behind us to give us shelter from the cold fingers of the wind. Bushes, bright with berries – there's food for us. Water here, to drink from and to bathe in. Huge stones, cast down from these mountains, for us to build our houses with, to make shelters for our animals, to wall us in. And below us… look! This rich valley for us to grow our crops, and to see from far away the approach of enemies.
Cai:	It is a good place. But… we must be sure…
Young Morgan:	I am sure. I know it. It's right for us, this field.
Olwen:	Please, Cai. I feel it too. This should be our home.
Cai:	You are right. We belong here. I see this field is good for you, Morgan. And Elen. And Olwen. May it always be good for our people, and for all who choose to live here. Come. Let us bless this earth.

Text 15 Interview with Jim Matthews

Jim Matthews is a poet and songwriter. He visited a school in Sunderland and talked to the children about his songwriting. They prepared some questions to ask him and afterwards wrote their conversation up in the form of an interview.

Class 5:	When did you begin writing songs?
Jim:	I started twenty-five years ago, just after I left school.
Class 5:	What made you want to become a songwriter?
Jim:	I always liked music, and when I was your age, I used to listen to the Beatles and wish I could write songs like them.
Class 5:	How do you decide on an idea for a song?
Jim:	From things that have happened to me, or people I've met, or things I've seen on the news – anything really.
Class 5:	What comes first – the words or the music?
Jim:	That depends; sometimes I'm tinkering around with some chords on my guitar and an idea comes to me. Or sometimes, I think of a phrase and build a song around that.
Class 5:	How long does it take you to write a song?
Jim:	Anything from ten minutes to two years. Some I started and never finished. You never know how long it's going to take.
Class 5:	Do you cross out and make lots of changes as you write?
Jim:	Yes, all the time.
Class 5:	What advice can you give to young songwriters?
Jim:	Write about the things that are important to you and don't give up. Keep trying!

Text 16 Homework Wizard

Tired of homework?

Is History driving you to distraction?

Does Mathematics tie you up in knots?

Well don't worry any longer

the new super deluxe

Homework Wizard **is here!**

This small, lightweight, easy to use, hand-held computer is the answer to all your problems. Internet compatible, it searches for the answers to your homework assignments in less time than it takes you to ask your parents! And it won't ask you to come back after it has finished reading the paper!)

The computer's amazing memory contains over five million facts, covering every topic of the National Curriculum, available to you at the touch of a button. Its cutting edge technology can save you time and tears.

Finished in sleek chrome with finger-friendly keys, the answer to your homework problems lies literally in your own hands.

Get one now, only £149.99

Available from all major electrical and department stores

Text 17a IslandBreeze Cruises

There's something happening virtually every hour of the day aboard *IslandBreeze*. To keep you up to speed, a copy of the Cruises News – a printed programme for the next day's activities – will be popped under your cabin door daily.

A typical day at sea might start with a gentle stretch-and-tone session on the Sun Deck; once you're limbered up, you could learn to Nashville line-dance with one of the ship's dancers. We'll make sure you know your way around the extensive equipment in the *IslandBreeze*'s gym, and that you don't get distracted by the unique view (you'll have to see it to appreciate it!).

After lunch you might be tempted to move indoors, where a host of activities are under way around the ship. There's a bridge tournament in the handsomely furnished Library/Card Room and a bingo session in one of the bars. The band's pianist challenges your ear with *Name That Tune*, while the Head Barman might be leading a 'mix-master' class (be sure to sample the ship's own speciality cocktails).

Choose Your Cabin

All *IslandBreeze* cabins are fully air-conditioned and have a fitted wardrobe, drawers, wall-to-wall carpeting, and en-suite facilities (shower, wc and hand-basin).

⚙ Superior

Superior class lets you enjoy your cruise on a higher deck, and generally in more spacious surroundings. A number of both inside and outside cabins have a third or fourth berth, making them most appealing to families. Some cabins with double beds are also available. Outside cabins all have a picture window or porthole.

⚙ Standard

All Standard cabins are tastefully furnished, with two lower beds; outside cabins have a porthole. Some cabins with a third and fourth upper berth are also available, and the *IslandBreeze* has quite a few cabins with double beds.

⚙ Two-berths

Two-berth cabins are great value for money if you don't plan on spending a lot of time in your cabin. Space for storage is limited; one bed is always an upper berth that folds down from the wall.

You're back on board from your excursion ashore; you've met friends for a relaxing sun-downer at The Pub; now you're ready for a delicious dinner and night 'on the town'. There's a fabulous musical revue on in the Piccadilly Theatre and a dance band playing in the Cordoba Lounge.

Don't Miss the Most Wonderful Water Experience Ever!
Ashton Newtown Water Park is here!
Grand Opening Night: Friday 20th June

Opened by up-and-coming pop star, Tasha Stafford, who will be giving away signed photographs.
The first 100 lucky customers will receive a signed copy of Tasha's new hit single, 'Splash!'

Surfers' paradise
- Practise your skills in our tidal pool
- Bodyboards available to hire
- Surf in safety

- Enjoy the relaxation of our **aromatherapy spa bath!**

Three Fantastic Flumes

- Elephant flume for under 8s
- Rapids – a tyre flume for the whole family to enjoy
- Niagara – a vertical drop slide for the very brave – dare you ride it?

- Join your friends in our **bubbling jacuzzi!**

After your swim, why not enjoy a cool drink or a speciality coffee in our **Poolside Bistro**? A range of snacks is also available at very reasonable prices.

Prices

Adult
Day pass: £5.00
Half day: £3.00

Children 5 to 16
Day pass: £2.50
Half day: £1.50

Family
(2 adults and up to 3 children)   £10.00

Under 5s: free

Opening times

	Monday–Saturday
Main pool and flumes:	10 a.m. to 8 p.m.
Spa bath and Jacuzzi:	11 a.m. to 1 p.m. then 5 p.m. to 8 p.m.
Surfing pool:	10 a.m. to 8 p.m. (with waves every 15 minutes)
	Sunday
All facilities:	10 a.m. to 5 p.m.
Toddlers session:	9 a.m. to 10 a.m.

GORGEOUS GEORGE GIVES GOAL GLUT

Grangetown Wanderers 4 Herrington Rovers 1

A four-goal bonanza from centre forward, George Fenwick, gave Grangetown Wanderers fans something to shout about last night. Playing to a crowd of 48,000, the Stratford Stadium was at fever pitch, as goal after goal thundered into the back of the net.

The first goal came after just three minutes. A careless kick-out from Matthews, the Herrington goalie, found the feet of Grangetown left back, Gary Loadman, whose superb cross to Fenwick made goal-scoring look easy. Herrington didn't know what had hit them when a Fenwick flick flew over their keeper in the 23rd minute. They managed to scramble an untidy goal back just on the edge of half time, from Watson, but in the second half, at 2-1 down, they never looked like coming back into the game.

The last two goals in the 65th and 88th minute were equally as impressive; the first starting from a long, dribbling run by Loadman, passing with pin-point accuracy to winger, 'Staff' Stafford, whose high cross found the head of Fenwick, lurking in the six yard box. The last goal was a screaming shot from 20 metres out.

It was a fantastic performance from George, in what is probably his last season in professional football. He has announced his plans to retire in May but, after last night, that might just change!

Fenwick freezes out the opposition

Grangetown Wanderers 4 Herrington Rovers 1

A cohesive team effort, with stellar performances from veteran centre forward, George Fenwick, and up-and-coming left-back, Gary Loadman, led Grangetown Wanderers to an impressive win last night at the Stratford Stadium, which was filled to its capacity.

The fans were treated to five goals; four from Fenwick, and a consolation goal for Herrington, who looked completely overshadowed and outplayed by on-form Wanderers. The first, after three minutes, was the result of a mistake by the Herrington goalkeeper, Matthews, who never looked comfortable last night. He has just returned after a back injury and may need a few more games to return to his usual reliable form.

The second goal, a well-placed lob, would have been unreachable for any keeper. The partnership of Loadman and Fenwick was a delight to watch; Loadman's ability to take the ball and wrong-foot his opponents, made him a difficult adversary. His pin-point accuracy in passing and crossing helped Fenwick, who has provisionally announced his retirement at the end of this season, to score four well-crafted goals, including a header in the 65th minute.

The night was rounded off with a powerful long shot, twelve minutes from time, from 15 metres out, sealing Herrington's disappointment and seeing them slip into the relegation zone, while Wanderers climb to fifth in the league.

Riches of the rainforest

The rainforests are scattered in a band across the Equator, but they are disappearing at an alarming rate.

Think of Aladdin's Cave, full of chests brimming with multicoloured jewels, riches beyond your wildest dreams …

To someone who studies plants or insects, animals or birds, the tropical rainforests of the world are one big Aladdin's Cave. Nowhere else is there such a rich mixture of life. Nowhere else contains so many secrets we have yet to discover, secrets that might cure illnesses or prevent disease, or perhaps provide new sources of food.

With so much to offer, it is an international disaster that the rainforests are being "eaten up" at such an alarming rate. Rainforests are being destroyed to make way for "civilized" man to grow crops, to provide timber, to "develop" the land. About half the world's rainforest has already gone.

We are losing species at an astonishing rate because of the destruction of the rainforests. About 50 a day, or one every half hour or so, disappears off the face of the earth forever. Each one plays some part in the balance of the rainforest.

Dolphins in danger

Dolphins, which have developed a special "friendship" with humans over the centuries, are also threatened by pollution and people. Thousands of dolphins are dying around Japan's coast as hunters cash in on the shortage of whale meat caused by the whaling ban. At least 130 000 more dolphins die each year by drowning when they get caught in tuna fishermen's nets. Greenpeace says only urgent action will save dolphins from extinction.

Global warming

The average temperature of the atmosphere has risen by 0.5°C since records began in 1860. Although this may seem a very small increase, it is much faster than at any time in the past.

Most of the world's water is found in the southern hemisphere. As sea can absorb more heat than land, the impact of global warming will be felt more in the northern hemisphere. The Arctic region may become about 8°C warmer by the year 2100. The ice that melts as a result will raise global sea levels by 60–100 cm. Vast areas would be flooded. Already, giant cracks in the ice have appeared and vast chunks, the size of counties, have broken off. It is estimated that a rise of 10°C would cause the Arctic region to break up. This would happen within 200 years if the present rate of warming continues.

He knew from the moment he walked inside the house that this was an inside job. An initial inspection of the garden had shown no footprints in the soil; no cracked twigs or branches; no sign of a forced entry. The criminals in this case had known exactly what they wanted and where to find it.

He approached the householder, Mrs Llewelyn and asked her to show him where the robbery had taken place. She led him to a bright, clean kitchen, gleaming with chrome appliances.

"Here," she said, " this is where it happened."

"Right, tell me in your own words, what you remember of the time leading to the discovery of the missing items."

"Well, it was four o'clock and two of my children had just returned home from school, hungry as usual, so they were eating cookies and drinking orange juice from the fridge. I thought they were eating too many cookies and they would spoil their tea, so I took away the jar and put it on top of that high cupboard over there, well out of reach."

He looked in the direction that she pointed, but could not see any signs of a cookie jar.

She continued, "I went to pay the milkman at the door and when I came back, the cookie jar had vanished along with my Deluxe Triple Chocochoc Cookies!"

"Would you say that you were houseproud, Mrs Llewellyn?"

"Oh yes, I work from an office in my home, so I like everything to be tidy."

He cast a well-trained eye around the kitchen, looking for tiny clues that a lesser detective might miss. He noticed a kitchen chair, slightly out of place; a chair that a small person might have used to climb on the sink top; a spatula left carelessly on the draining board; spatulas were good for reaching hard-to-get things on tops of cupboards, and a tea towel that had been tightly scrunched up, as if someone had been trying to open a tight jar. But most telling of all, was a fine dusting of crumbs on the laminate flooring. Mrs Llewellyn had confirmed that she was a tidy person, she would not have left crumbs lying, so they must have been left by the criminals.

"I thought as much," he mused. "I think we're on to something! Wait here, Mrs Llewellyn, I think this case is about to be solved!"

His efforts to follow the crumb trail were vaguely hampered by Scruff, the family's pet dog, who was keen to eat the evidence. However, he was able to follow the choc chips up the stairs to the bedroom of the eldest child. He knocked commandingly on the door. From inside the room could be heard scuffling noises, as if someone was hiding something in a hurry.

"Open up!" he demanded, "I know you're in there!"

The door opened slowly and two guilty faces appeared in the opening; the aroma of chocolate was strong, they couldn't deny it, they had been caught red-handed!

Firmly, he spoke, "You two, Mum's going ballistic! She knows you've got the cookie jar and if you don't eat your tea you're going to be in real trouble! And thanks a bunch for not saving me any *and* eating them in *my* bedroom!"

Stefi and Rhys looked sheepishly at their elder brother. He walked away down the stairs with the cookie jar in his hand. Another case solved for this fearless detective.

Sir Arthur Conan Doyle (May 22nd 1859 – July 7th 1930)

Arthur Conan Doyle was born in England in Victorian times and trained in medicine, working as a ship's doctor, then as a doctor in Plymouth and Southsea. He is famous for inventing the world-famous detective, Sherlock Holmes, who first appeared in the book, *A Study in Scarlet* in 1887. He killed off the character in 1893, sending him over a waterfall with his arch-enemy, Moriarty, but due to public demand, he brought the character back to life, saying he had managed to climb back up the cliff!

Sherlock Holmes

Sherlock Holmes specialized in solving difficult crimes through observation and deduction. People came to his house in London's Baker Street to ask for his help. His name came from the surnames of two cricketers: Sherlock and Holmes.
He was always assisted by his friend, Dr. Watson, who often narrated the stories. Sherlock Holmes was famous for his deerstalker hat, his pipe smoking and his ability to play the violin.

Agatha Christie (September 15th 1890 – January 12th 1976)

Agatha Christie was a British crime writer, born in Torquay, who published over 80 books, mainly 'whodunits'. She invented two famous literary detectives: Miss Marple and Hercule Poirot. Many of her books have been made into television programmes and films. During World War 1, she worked as a pharmacist, which gave her information about poisons to refer to in her writing, and in 1926, she caused her own mystery by disappearing for 11 days.

Miss Marple

Jane Marple is an amateur detective who lives in the village of St. Mary Mead. She does not look like the typical detective as she is an elderly lady dressed in tweed and a hat but, in her stories, she often outwits the police with her sharp mind and her ability to piece the evidence together. Witnesses talk to her easily as she looks like everyone's idea of a favourite granny!

Hercule Poirot

Hercule Poirot was a Belgian policeman, invented by Agatha Christie, who moved to Britain after World War 1, where he became a private detective. He is famous for his moustache, his smart suits and his use of his "little grey cells". He has a partner, Arthur Hastings, who helps him to solve cases. His most famous case is probably, 'Murder on the Orient Express'.

Colin Dexter (September 29th 1930–)

Colin Dexter was born in Stamford, Lincolnshire. He studied at Cambridge University but then moved to Oxford in 1966. He started writing after a holiday to Wales in 1972. It was wet and he read two mystery novels to pass the time. He decided he could write better books, so he invented the hugely popular character, Inspector Morse. Many of Colin Dexter's books have been made into a long-running TV series, starring John Thaw in the title role.

Inspector Morse

Inspector Morse solves crimes in the Oxford area. His first name, Endeavour, was kept secret until nearly the last novel. He was helped in his detective work by his sidekick, Sergeant Lewis. Morse is famous for his Jaguar car, his passion for opera and classical music and beer. The character was killed off in the last novel, *The Remorseful Day*, in 2000. Unlike Sherlock Holmes, Colin Dexter has no plans to bring his character back to life!

Dorothy L. Sayers (13th June 1893 – 17th December 1957)
Dorothy L. Sayers (she insisted on the L. being included) was a British author and translator. She was born in Oxford and was one of the first women to receive a degree from Oxford University. Dorothy worked as a teacher and as an advertising copywriter. She is most famous for inventing the detective Lord Peter Wimsey. She also wrote short stories about another character, Montague Egg, a wine salesman who also solves mysteries.

Lord Peter Wimsey
Lord Peter Wimsey is an aristocrat who solves murder mysteries in the 1920s to 1940s. He has an assistant, his manservant, Bunter, who is at least as talented as Wimsey. Lord Peter is also helped by his wife, Harriet Vane, who is a crime writer. Wimsey is famous for his love of food, his piano and his Daimler car, which he calls "Mrs Merdle'" after a character in a Charles Dickens book.

Text 22 Becoming a Reading Detective

Biblio Magazine interviewed writer, Claire Roberts, about her views on children and reading.

Biblio: Welcome, Claire. You've just had an article published in a major national newspaper, in which you called for children to become 'reading detectives'. Can you tell me what you meant by this?

Claire: I was trying to get across the idea that, when we read, we are piecing together all sorts of information, just like a detective, in order to understand and get the most out of what we are reading.

Biblio: So can anyone become a reading detective? How do you go about becoming one?

Claire: Well, it's about reading carefully and using everything on the page to help you understand the text: if there are pictures, look for clues in them, like a detective would view a crime scene. If you don't understand a word, look it up or ask an adult; detectives use other experts to help them solve a case. I have a dictionary and a thesaurus on my desk all the time. I also write interesting words in a notebook, to use in my own writing, just like a detective makes notes to use later.

Biblio: What if you're not a very good reader?

Claire: Everyone has to start somewhere. Ask your teacher or parents for extra help. Join your school reading club, if there is one, and read lots and lots of different things. The more you read, the easier it gets!

Biblio: Does it matter what you read?

Claire: Some people think you can only improve your reading through books, but we use reading in our everyday lives as well. For example, we read: road signs, text messages, labels, menus, shopping lists, letters, e-mails, posters and postcards, not to mention newspapers, magazines and comics! But I think the key thing is to read a variety of material, including books. The more you read, the more often you will meet unusual words and get to know what they mean.

Biblio: Claire, thank you very much for coming in. I hope you can inspire a generation of reading detectives

ANALYSING INTERVIEWS

What you need to know

1 Know and recall the features of an interview.

2 Know the difference between the interviewer and interviewee.

3 Understand the difference between open and closed questions.

THE FEATURES OF AN INTERVIEW

- An interview is a planned conversation, usually between two people, in which one person asks questions (the **interviewer**) and the other answers them (the **interviewee**).

- The interviewer controls the interview by directing the questions and also by responding to information given by the interviewee.

- Interviews are set out in a similar way to a play, with a new line for each new speaker.

Quick tip

As an interview is a conversation, Standard English does not always have to be used.

Interviewer:	Today I am speaking to Vera Patchett, world cross-stitch champion, on her amazing achievements. Tell me, Vera, when did you first take up this hobby?
Vera Patchett:	Oh, I've been sewing since I was a little girl.
Interviewer:	And when did you realize that you were so good at it?
Vera Patchett:	I think it was while I was at secondary school, when I embroidered the school badge on the football team's strips. Then people wanted me to sew pictures of pop stars on their jackets and school bags. It made me very popular!

OPEN AND CLOSED QUESTIONS

Interviewers vary the kinds of questions asked to keep the interview interesting. Questions may be open or closed.

- **Open questions** allow the interviewee to talk more and express opinions.

Tell me about your childhood
Why do you think you have been so successful?
What was it like the first time you appeared on stage?

Interviewers try to use lots of this type of question.

- **Closed questions** are simple questions that require only a 'yes' or 'no' answer, or a very short answer.

How old are you?   Do you like golf?

If an interview was made up of only these kinds of questions, it would be very boring and you wouldn't find out much about the interviewee.

ANALYSING INTERVIEWS

1 Read Text 15: Interview with Jim Matthews.

(a) Why are the names of the interviewer and interviewee on the left hand side of the page, in front of the words they say?

_____

(b) When did Jim Matthews start writing songs?

_____

(c) Is the first question an open or a closed question?

_____

(d) Find and write down **one** open question used in this interview.

_____

(e) From where does Jim Matthews say he gets his ideas?

_____

2 Think of **three** more open-ended questions Class 5 could have asked Jim Matthews.

(i) _____

(ii) _____

(iii) _____

3 What do you think the word 'tinkering' means?

_____

_____

4 Why does Jim say he never knows how long it will take to write a song?

_____

_____

_____

WRITING INTERVIEWS

What you need to know

1 Know and recall the features of an interview.

2 Plan a series of questions suitable for an interview.

FEATURES OF A GOOD INTERVIEW

- An **interview** often starts with an introduction, saying who the **interviewee** is and why they are being interviewed. This helps to set the scene.

- Before an interview, the interviewer will research their interviewee, finding out things to make an interesting interview (e.g. birthplace, interests, achievements so far), and ask the interviewee questions on those subjects.

PLANNING FOR AN INTERVIEW

- An **interviewer** plans the questions they are going to ask an interviewee. They may not always stick to their planned questions, as the interviewee may give some interesting information that leads the interview in a different direction.

Interview Planning Sheet

Name of interviewee:
What they are famous for/why I am interviewing them:
My opening question will be:
Other questions I would like to ask: • • • • • • • •
I will end my interview like this:

To get a successful interview you need to ask mainly open questions.

Quick tip

To be a good interviewer, you need to be a good listener and let the interviewee speak without butting in!

Useful phrases

Tell me about …

How did you …

What have you learnt from …

Why did you …

Looking back over your achievements …

When did you realise …

What are your hopes for the future? …

WRITING INTERVIEWS

1 Which of the following are open and which are closed questions?
Write **open** or **closed** at the end of each question.

(a) How old are you? _____

(b) What can you tell me about your schooldays? _____

(c) Why do you think you have been so successful? _____

(d) Do you like writing? _____

(e) What are your hopes for the future? _____

2 Here are some closed questions. Rewrite them as open questions.
You will need to add some words and rearrange the sentences.

(a) Did you have a happy childhood?

_____

(b) How many books have you written?

_____

(c) What is the title of your next book?

_____

(d) Do you find it easy to think of new ideas?

_____

(e) Do you like being a writer?

_____

3 Plan a short interview with someone you know, about his or her favourite book.

Think about the kind of questions you will ask. Carry out the interview
with a couple of your friends, your parents or your grandparents and
see what their answers are. It might be interesting to compare them!

4 Choose any person (alive, dead or fictional) who interests you.
Carefully plan an interview with this person and write down the questions you
would like to ask them.
Then write up your imaginary interview in your writer's notebook.
Let someone else read it and tell you what they think about it.

SPELLING: PLURALS

What you need to know

1 Understand the term 'plural'.

2 Know how to write the correct endings for common plural forms.

COMMON PLURAL ENDINGS

Most plurals are made by adding **s** to the end of a word.	barbecue**s** bicycle**s** cat**s** curtain**s** dog**s** dog**s** duvet**s** elephant**s** eraser**s** fiddle**s** house**s** lollipop**s** onion**s** partition**s** road**s** sieve**s** station**s** sweet**s** tube**s**
When a word ends in **s** or **h**, add **es**.	birch**es** crash**es** dish**es** flash**es** glass**es** match**es** peach**es** speech**es**
If a word ends in **y**, change the **y** to an **i** and add **es**, e.g. **cherry → cherries**.	bab**ies** broll**ies** bab**ies** dair**ies** dais**ies** diar**ies** fair**ies** foll**ies** jell**ies** loll**ies** lorr**ies** pans**ies**
However, if the word ends in **ey**, add an **s** to make the plural, e.g. **monkey → monkeys**.	chimney**s** chutney**s** monkey**s** trolley**s** valley**s**
When a word ends in **f**, change the **f** to a **v** and add **es**, e.g. **thief → thieves**.	cal**ves** hal**ves** hoo**ves** scar**ves** thie**ves** wol**ves** (**hoofs** and **scarfs** are also acceptable **but** roof is always **roofs**)

Quick tip

A plural is more than one of something e.g **one car → two cars**.

ODD ONES OUT

- Of course there are exceptions to the rule. The following words change like this to make their plural:

man → men

woman → women

child → children

mouse → mice

person → people

sheep → sheep

deer → deer

If house becomes houses,
Why aren't mice mouses?
Boot becomes boots,
So why aren't feet foots!
There's just no way of telling,
When I'll get the hang of spelling!

SPELLING: PLURALS

1 Put the correct endings on the following words to make their plural forms.

monkey	➜ _____	house	➜ _____	
party	➜ _____	scarf	➜ _____	
valley	➜ _____	wolf	➜ _____	
crash	➜ _____	diary	➜ _____	
baby	➜ _____	half	➜ _____	
elephant	➜ _____			

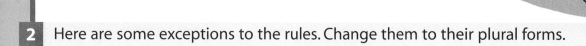

2 Here are some exceptions to the rules. Change them to their plural forms.

child	➜ _____	woman	➜ _____
person	➜ _____	sheep	➜ _____
mouse	➜ _____	man	➜ _____

3 Here is your spelling test for plural words.

Remember: Look, Cover, Write, Check.

	1st attempt	2nd attempt	3rd attempt
lorries			
chimney			
houses			
speeches			
dairies			
calves			
people			
women			
children			
halves			
entries			
glasses			

ANALYSING PERSUASIVE WRITING

What you need to know

1 Understand what is meant by persuasive writing.

2 Know the main features of persuasive writing.

ADVERTISEMENTS

- Everyday examples of **persuasive writing** are the advertisements that you see in newspapers and magazines and on television.

- Choice of words is really important when writing persuasively. The **advertisers** want to sell their product, so they choose words that will make us buy them.

exclusive

only

unbelievable offer

new improved

unique

state of the art

Remember
Persuasive writing is aimed at getting the reader to accept the writer's point of view or persuading the reader to do something.

You need to use words like these in your persuasive writing.

BIASED WRITING

- When you are reading advertisements and other persuasive writing, it is important to realize that this kind of writing is **biased**. This means that the writer is only putting forward the good points and not mentioning any bad points, in order to persuade you. **For example**, in an advert for a mobile phone, they may tell you how cheap it is to text someone, but they may not tell you how expensive it is to phone someone during the day!

- Alternatively, if someone feels strongly about something, they may only put forward their own point of view and not a **balanced argument**. So, when you are reading persuasive writing, read it carefully and try to think not only about what the writer is telling you but also about what they are not telling you!

YOUR POINT OF VIEW

- Persuasive writing can also be used to make somebody see your point of view or to make them give in to your requests. **For example**, if you felt strongly about a subject, such as foxhunting, or school dinners, you could write to your local newspaper or MP, expressing your point of view. You would have to write your points clearly, using **Standard English**, and use persuasive language.

Quick tip

Collect examples of persuasive writing and stick them in your writer's notebook.

I'm sure you will agree...   In view of the facts...

There can be only one answer.

ANALYSING PERSUASIVE WRITING

1 Read Text 6a: The letter to the editor of the Langfield Echo.

(a) What is Mrs Barrass complaining about?

_____

_____

(b) Find **two** statements in the letter which are biased (Mrs Barrass' opinion, not fact).

(i) _____

(ii) _____

(c) What **two** things is Mrs Barrass hoping to persuade people to do?

(i) _____

(ii) _____

(d) Write down the meanings of the following words:

ever-present _____

vulnerable _____

obscuring _____

2 Read Text 16: the advertisement for the Homework Wizard.

(a) Write down **two** features of the Homework Wizard.

(i) _____

(ii) _____

(b) Find **two** ways the advertisers are trying to persuade you to buy one.

(i) _____

(ii) _____

(c) Who do you think this advertisement is aimed at?

_____

(d) Find some evidence in the text to back up your opinion.

_____

WRITING PERSUASIVELY

What you need to know

1 Plan and write pieces of persuasive writing.

PLANNING

Planning a persuasive letter

My letter is about:

I will begin like this:

The main points I want to get across are:

-
-
-
-
-

Phrases I might use:

I will end my letter like this:

Planning an advertisement or poster

My advertisement/poster is about:

The main features/good points are:

-
-
-
-
-

Words and phrases I might use:

My snappy slogan will be:

Useful phrases

I'm sure you will agree

there is only one course of action

all things considered

undoubtedly

without exception

in my opinion

as soon as possible

I hope you will do your utmost

it is undeniably true

the importance of this cannot be overestimated

it is up to us all

join with me in

your help would be greatly appreciated

thank you for letting me air my views

Remember
When you are doing persuasive writing your word choice is very important. You are trying to make people see your point of view or make them buy something.

Add a slogan
When you are writing advertisements, think of a snappy slogan, a short phrase that makes your product memorable.

57

WRITING PERSUASIVELY

1 The council has just decided to take away your school crossing patrol officer in order to save money. Imagine you are one of the parents. On a separate piece of paper, write a persuasive letter to your local council protesting about this decision.

Talk about:
• the safety of young children
• the amount of traffic passing your school
• the lack of safe places to cross near your school
• the feelings of the other parents.

2 The school caterers want more children to buy school lunches.
Design a poster or advertisement that will persuade more children to buy school lunches.

• Emphasize the healthy-eating aspect of a balanced diet that school lunches offer.
• Use persuasive vocabulary.
• Try writing short, snappy slogans.
• Look back at the advert for the 'Homework Wizard' for ideas.
• Set out your work out in an eye-catching and attractive way.
• Can you invent a character to help get your message across?

ANALYSING LEAFLETS AND BROCHURES

What you need to know

1 Understand the main features of leaflets and brochures.

2 Gain examples of the kind of language used in leaflets and brochures.

LEAFLETS AND BROCHURES

- **Leaflets** and **brochures** are primarily designed to **inform**, but are also intended to **persuade**.

Think of all the places that you might find advertising leafets and brochures.

Leaflets: advertising museums, art galleries, swimming baths, outdoor centres, etc.

Holiday brochures: to tempt you to visit a particular hotel, resort or country.

Your school may have a brochure which is given to parents to inform them about all the good things your school has to offer.

Can you think of any more?

Quick tip

The layout of leaflets and brochures is very important. Collect examples to see how they have been put together.

FEATURES OF LEAFLETS AND BROCHURES

- Leaflets and brochures are used for lots of different purposes, but they contain many of the same features.

The name of the place or product is clearly written and repeated.

Information is given about opening times, prices, location etc.

Information is given about the **facilities** of a building or resort, or the **functions** and **features** of a machine or appliance.

Pictures are often used to give more information, or to add appeal.

Sometimes **quotations** are used from satisfied customers, saying how good the product or place is.

Special offers, or reduced prices (called concessions).

Telephone helpline numbers, or information numbers and web addresses, are often included.

ANALYSING LEAFLETS AND BROCHURES

1 Read Text 17a: *IslandBreeze Cruises*, an extract from a holiday brochure.

(a) How are passengers informed of the following day's activities?

_____

(b) Which cabin would you prefer and why? _____

(c) Suggest **three** activities you could take part in during the day.

(i) _____

(ii) _____

(iii) _____

2 Read Text 17b about Ashton Newtown Water Park, a new amenity for the public.

(a) What is the purpose of this leaflet?

_____

(b) Between which times could you have a spa bath on Sunday? _____

(c) Why do you think Tasha Stafford was chosen to open the baths?

_____

(d) Name **two** different activities available in Ashton Newtown Water Park.

(i) _____

(ii) _____

(e) How much does it cost for a half-day pass for a child of 11? _____

(f) When advertising the Niagara Flume, why do you think the writer says, "Dare you ride it?"

_____

_____

(g) If you were visiting the Water Park, which **two** activities would you most like to do and why?

(i) _____

(ii) _____

60

LEAFLETS AND BROCHURES

What you need to know

1 Plan and write in the style of a leaflet or brochure.

BEFORE YOU START

- Plan all the information you want to include in your brochure.

- Think about who your leaflet or brochure is aimed at (e.g. young children, teenagers or adults) and write accordingly.

YOUR PLAN

My leaflet/brochure is about:	Useful words and phrases I might use are:
My target audience is (who my writing is aimed at):	
The main pieces of information I want to write are: • • • • • •	

Useful words and phrases

Once in a lifetime opportunity

only available to selected customers

exclusive

Only

SPECIAL OFFER

relax in peaceful surroundings

free child places

place of historic interest

place of outstanding natural beauty

Quick tip

When you have written your leaflet or brochure, read it through and see if you can understand it. If it's not clear to you, it won't be clear to anyone else!

If you find any more phrases you like using, write them in your writer's notebook.

LEAFLETS AND BROCHURES

You will need your writer's notebook, or some sheets of A4 paper, for these activities.

1 Design a leaflet for your local Wildfowl Park, which is called 'Feathered Friends'. The centre has just reopened after improvements, which now include: toilets and ramps for the disabled, a new cafeteria, a souvenir shop, a classroom for school visits and an adventure playground.
The centre also provides guided tours by experts, with feeding sessions for ducks and gulls, a daily falconry display, as well as having one of the largest collections of owls in the country. The cost of a visit is £4.50 per adult and £2.50 per child, with a family ticket for two adults and up to four children which costs £12.00. Opening times are from 9 a.m. until dusk, seven days a week.

- Put as much information into the brochure as you can.
- Use impersonal and persuasive words to encourage people to go.
- Emphasize the wonderful facilities and suggest how Feathered Friends would make a good day out for all the family.

2 Write a report for a holiday brochure about the town, city or village that you live in.

- Include three places of interest that visitors to your area could see, or three activities that visitors could take part in.
- If you have pictures or photographs (you could cut some out of your local newspaper), add them to your brochure to make it look more authentic.
- Add some 'quotations' by interviewing your friends and family and including their comments.
- Find out and include opening times and prices, if possible.
- Look at a map and describe the locations of your places of interest.

SPELLING: VOWEL DIGRAPHS

What you need to know

1 Learn and use words containing vowel digraphs.

VOWEL DIGRAPHS

- When two vowels are put together in a word, they have a sound that is unlike the two short vowel sounds. **For example**, the 'i' and 'e' in believe, or the 'e' and 'i' in receive.

- These blended vowels are called **vowel digraphs**. They may look the same but they don't always sound the same in words:

  Are you going to read that book?

  Have you read that book?

Some words containing vowel digraphs:

ai	curtain captain bargain waist chain frail explain contain
au	cautious clause applaud laundry autumn saucer automatic
ea	read heat thread bear lead
ei	reign weight neighbour height neither ceiling receipt perceive
ie	believe niece achieve thief priest fierce shriek view sieve
oa	cocoa coax loathe approach
oe	echoes potatoes tomatoes
oi	choice avoid moisture rejoice spoil noisy
ou	spout pronounce bough discourage couple honour wound youth
ue	guess guest fatigue vague league argue
ui	juice nuisance suit guide build guitar penguin guilty

'I' BEFORE 'E'

- Here is a very useful rule to remember which order to write 'i' and 'e' in words:

  'i' before 'e', except after 'c'.

  This means that, in most words, when 'i' and 'e' are present together, the 'e' is written after the 'i', except when the letter 'c' precedes them:

  th**ie**f **but** c**ei**ling.

- An exception to the rule is **their**, when 'e' comes before 'i'.

SPELLING: VOWEL DIGRAPHS

1 Fill in the blanks in the following words with either **ei** or **ie**. Remember: 'i' **before** 'e'.

fr___nd   c___ling   n___ther   th___f   f___ld

n___ce   rec___pt   dec___ve   pr___st   ch___f

2 Read the clues to complete the words below. Each word contains a vowel digraph.

(a) Cotton to sew with   th_____
(b) To clap your hands   a_____
(c) A season   a_____
(d) The people who live next door   n_____
(e) To hurt someone   w_____
(f) An Antarctic bird   p_____
(g) Person in charge of a ship   c_____
(h) Stay away from   a_____
(i) Vegetables which may be mashed, fried or boiled p_____

3 Find 15 vowel digraph words in this wordsearch.

echoes	juice	belief
cocoa	couple	unchain
haul	waist	moisture
reign	height	vault
roast	eight	believe

e	c	h	o	e	s	h	b	h	x
f	o	e	l	r	y	r	e	e	l
o	c	j	i	n	b	e	e	i	j
c	o	u	p	l	e	i	l	g	r
d	a	i	y	w	l	g	e	h	o
u	n	c	h	a	i	n	a	t	a
g	b	e	l	i	e	f	g	r	s
h	a	u	l	s	v	a	u	l	t
e	i	g	h	t	e	h	e	m	d
d	m	o	i	s	t	u	r	e	p

4 Write out 10 of the words you found in your wordsearch in the Spelling chart below. They will be the words to learn for this week's spelling test.

Remember to Look, Cover, Write, Check as usual.

	1st attempt	2nd attempt	3rd attempt

NEWSPAPER REPORTS

What you need to know

1 Understand the main features of newspaper reports.

2 Distinguish between biased and objective newspaper reports.

FEATURES

- Newspapers need to catch the reader's attention so people will want to buy the paper. In order to do this, journalists write short, snappy and attention-grabbing **headlines**, saying in a few words, what the story is about.

LOTTERY MILLIONAIRE IS GIVING IT AWAY!

FIREWORK FIASCO!

BECKHAM BLINDER BEATS BORO'

HOWZAT!

COW WON'T MOO-VE, CAUSES MAYHEM

- **Alliteration** is often used:

  Boy badly bruised from building fall.

- Sometimes a **pun** (a word joke) is used to achieve this, such as 'cow won't moo've'.

- Journalistic writing is usually arranged in short lines called **columns**.

- **Subheadings** are used to introduce different sections of the main topic.

STYLE

- Look at the styles of different newspapers.
  Some use a lot of pictures and competitions to grab your attention. They may use words like:

  Wow! What a scorcher!

  Others are more serious in style and report on important news stories, such as what has happened in Parliament. The language in these papers tends to be more serious, too. Different newspapers are written for different audiences and you must find the style that suits you best.

BIAS

- You have to read newspapers carefully. If you bought two papers, the same story might be in each, but the detail may have changed, or some of the facts may be different. This is because more information becomes available as a story progresses, different witnesses see things in different ways or the article may be **biased**; this means that it is written from one point of view, not in a balanced way, or **objective** way.

GORGEOUS GEORGE GIVES GOAL GLUT

1 Read texts 18a and b: two articles, from different types of newspaper.

   (a) What was the score at the end of the match? _____

   (b) Who scored the goals for both teams?

   _____

   (c) When did Herrington score their only goal? _____

   (d) Why is this an important football season for George Fenwick?

   _____

   (e) What is the name of the Grangetown left-back? _____

   (f) Why might the Herrington goal keeper not have been on his best form?

   _____

2 Text 18a uses dramatic and emotional words such as 'thundered', 'bonanza', 'screaming shot', 'fever pitch'. What is the effect of using these kinds of words?

_____

3 Text 18b gives a more serious and less emotional description of events. It uses some less-familiar words. Can you find another word similar in meaning to each of these words?

stellar _____   adversary _____   consolation _____

4 Look at the two articles (texts 18a and b).

   (a) Of the two reports, which style do you prefer? Give reasons for your choice.

   _____

   _____

   _____

   (b) Think of a suitable headline of your own for each of these articles.

   _____

   _____

WRITING A NEWSPAPER REPORT

What you need to know

1 Write in the style of a newspaper reporter.

FEATURES OF JOURNALISTIC WRITING

- Articles are usually written in this form:

  they start with a headline to grab attention,
  followed by a short outline of the main points of the story,
  then an expansion of the story, written in paragraphs.

- Journalistic writing should tell the reader when, where, what and why an event happened and who was involved.

- If possible, quotes are taken from witnesses or people involved in the story to make it more interesting.

A Planning Frame

I am writing an article about:
My ideas for a headline are:
When did it take place?
Where did it happen?
Who was involved?
What happened? • • • • • • •
Why/How did it happen?
I will use these quotes to make my story more interesting:
I will end my article like this:

Quick tips

- You are not writing a story. Don't write, "I did..." and put yourself into the report. Write it as if you had watched the event happening as a witness or observer. Read different newspapers to get used to their style.
- Use paragraphs.
- Use impersonal vocabulary, such as:

  The robbery took place...
  The crash occurred...
  The event was witnessed by...
  It is hoped that...
  It seems to have been...

- Avoid overused words such as 'good', 'bad' and 'exciting'. Use a thesaurus to help you choose alternatives.
- Journalistic writing should be objective. Stick to the facts.
- Journalistic writing should always attempt to entertain the reader, whether its purpose is to inform, instruct or persuade.

Check

- Has your article got an attention-grabbing headline that is relevant to the article?
- Does your article read like a newspaper report and not a story?
- Have you answered the questions: when, where, who, what and why?

WRITING A NEWSPAPER REPORT

You will need your writer's notebook, or some sheets of A4 paper, for these activities.

1 Look at the list of stories reported in a newspaper.

(a) Write a catchy headline and the opening sentence of a newspaper article for each of the events below:

- the first person to land on Mars
- a family who wins the lottery jackpot
- survivors of an earthquake
- a snake escaping from the local zoo
- a school child who finds a Roman coin in their garden.

Daily News

SPACE BALLOONISTS TRAGEDY

As a misty dawn broke over the coast, the extent of the damage became apparent

(b) Now choose **one** of your openings to write in the newspaper mock-up below:

Daily News

2 Read Texts 18a and b (the two football articles) again.
Write an article about a sporting event, real or imaginary.
Write it in the style of the first article about the football match.

Include an interesting headline (perhaps with alliteration or a pun) and a brief summary of the event using exciting, dramatic and emotional words.
You may find it helpful to use the journalistic writing Planning Frame on page 67.

3 Write a newspaper article about something that has happened in your school or local area.

Interview some people involved, so that you can make the report sound authentic (real).
Make it as interesting as possible and think of a snappy headline!

BIAS

What you need to know

1 Identify and understand the main features of report writing.

2 Understand the need for a factual report or argument to be balanced rather than biased.

MAIN FEATURES OF A REPORT

- Reports are often organized in this way.

the title → Should children get homework?

→ an introductory paragraph outlining the subject of the report

the main part of the report, written in paragraphs, often with sub-headings to divide up the different sections of text (This makes it clearer for the reader to follow and helps them to find particular information in a text.)

→ pictures, diagrams or maps are often included to give extra detail and make reports easier to understand

Summary

a final paragraph, going over the main points of the report again

Remember
Your own writing should, unless its content is extremely serious, attract the reader's attention by being entertaining.

BALANCED NOT BIASED

- A **balanced argument** often presents possible answers to a question for which there is likely to be more than one point of view.

  Should foxhunting be banned?   Should children get homework?

  Are there too many cars on the road?

- In a balanced argument, both sides are given, without **bias** (the writer's opinion) in order to let the reader make up their own mind on the issue.

- At the end of a balanced argument, there is often a **summary**, which is a recap of the main points for and against the argument. This allows readers a further opportunity to weigh up the evidence.

STYLE

- Not all writing is like a story: **reports**, leaflets and other information documents have their own styles and vocabularies.

- They use impersonal, objective language.

  it would seem   it is generally thought   some people believe...

- Subheadings are used to introduce different sections of the main topic.

BIAS

1 Read text 19: 'A Changing World', an information text, taken from a reference book.

(a) Is this extract a balanced argument or is it someone's opinion based on facts?

_____

(b) Why has the writer used subheadings in this report?

_____

(c) Why does the writer use the term 'Aladdin's Cave' to describe the rainforests?

_____

_____

(d) In 'Riches of the Rainforest', the words 'civilized' and 'develop' are written in inverted commas. Why do you think the writer has used inverted commas?

_____

2 (a) Which **two** factors are threatening the safety of dolphins?

(i) _____

(ii) _____

(b) When you read this report, how does it make you feel? Use **three** adjectives to describe your reaction.

_____   _____   _____

(c) How has the writer made you feel this way? Explain as fully as you can, using parts of the text to support your opinion.

_____

_____

3 (a) Name **three** things that may happen as a result of global warming.

(i) _____

(ii) _____

(iii) _____

(b) Using information from all the articles, write a short paragraph saying what the author believes the effect will be on our planet and its species if things go on as they are now.

_____

_____

WRITING A BALANCED ARGUMENT

What you need to know

1 Plan and write a report.

2 Plan and write a balanced argument.

REPORT WRITING

- Report writing is factual, uses mainly impersonal writing, but may be biased in favour of the writer's opinion.
  The writer will use facts to back up their point of view.

Reporter's Planning Frame

- What is my report about?
- Who is my writing intended for (e.g. children or adults)?
- What are my key points?
- How shall I organize my writing? (Shall I use bullets or numbers?)
- Will I use subheadings? What will they be?
- Are there any special words and phrases that I might use?
- How will I end my piece?

> **Remember**
> Use impersonal language and use the present tense. Think about organizing your report into smaller sections with subheadings. Include pictures, if you can, to add extra detail to your report.

BALANCED ARGUMENTS

- Balanced arguments are like written discussions, in which both sides of the argument are presented in a clear and unbiased way, allowing the reader to weigh up the evidence and come to their own conclusions.

- When writing a balanced argument, remember to:

  organize the two sides of your argument into a balanced report

  start with an introductory paragraph outlining the argument

  list the points in favour of the argument, alternating them with the points against the argument

  sum up the main points at the end.

Planning a balanced argument

- The subject I am discussing is:
- I will start my argument like this:
- The points in favour of the argument are:
- The points against the argument are:
- I will sum up my argument like this:

> **Check**
> - Have you used mainly impersonal language?
> - Have you organized your writing into paragraphs?
> - Have you used facts to back up your opinion in the report?
> - Have you started and ended with the main points in your balanced argument?

WRITING A BALANCED ARGUMENT

You will need your writer's notebook, or some sheets of A4 paper, for these activities.

1 Write an informative report on looking after a pet of your choice.

- Your article should contain advice on feeding, exercise, living conditions, bedding, play, veterinary care and grooming.

- Give advice on the suitability of the pet for different houses, e.g. a flat, a house with a garden, or a house near a busy road, as well as its suitability for people of different ages, e.g. a young child, or an old lady.

- Write about the good things and the bad things about looking after a pet.

2 Write a balanced report about whether children need playtimes in school.

Possible points in favour could be:

- it gives children a time to relax

- it allows children to get fresh air

- it gives children the opportunity to exercise

- it allows children to mix and talk with their friends.

Possible points against could be:

- it disrupts lessons

- children lose concentration

- there isn't enough to do outside

- school could finish earlier if there were no playtimes.

Add some more points of your own.

Use the box opposite to plan your report.

SPELLING: PREFIXES AND SUFFIXES

What you need to know

1 Learn the spelling of commonly used prefixes and suffixes and understand their meanings.

A PLETHORA OF PREFIXES

- **Prefixes** are groups of letters that go in front of a word to make a new word. Each prefix has a meaning that you will need to learn.

aero (air)	aerodrome aerodynamic aeronaut aeroplane
aqua (water)	aquaduct aquaplane aquarium aquatic
audi (hearing/listening)	audible audience audition auditorium
auto (self)	autobiography autograph automatic automobile
hydra (water)	hydrant hydrate hydraulic
hydro (water)	hydroelectric hydrofoil hydroplane
photo (light)	photograph photosynthesis
tele (distance)	telegram telegraph telephone telescope television
trans (across/through)	transaction transfer transparent transplant transport

- These prefixes make words into negative forms:

il- illogical	**im-** imbalance	**in-** inattentive
ir- irresponsible	**un-** undo	

- More prefixes

anti-, bio-, de-, dis-, ex-, im-, in-, il-, ir-, magni-, micro-, post-, pre-, pro-, re-, sub-, super-, un-

A SELECTION OF SUFFIXES

- **Suffixes** are groups of letters that go on the end of a word to make a new word. Many suffixes have meanings that would be helpful for you to learn.

-graph (writing)	autograph photograph pictograph telegraph
-ology (study of)	archaeology biology geology zoology
-phobia (fear of)	agoraphobia arachnophobia claustrophobia
-ian	electrician Grecian magician
-ion	completion confession confusion devotion exclusion obsession pollution possession station superstition

Can you find a rule for which words take -ian and which take -ion?
Which words take -tion and which take -sion?
Look in a dictionary to find what the words using the above prefixes and suffixies mean.

- More suffixes

-able, -ette, -ful, -ic, -ible, -ive, -less, -meter, -naut, -y

Quick tip

When -ful appears as a suffix, it has only one 'l'. This catches a lot of people out.

73

SPELLING: PREFIXES AND SUFFIXES

1 Add the correct suffix, **-ible** or **-able,** to the end of each of these words.

fashion_____   imposs_____   respons_____   question_____   valu_____

unthink_____   horr_____   change_____   divis_____   like_____

Can you spot any rules for which words take which suffix?

-ible _____

-able _____

2 Which of these prefixes make sense at the beginnings of the following words?

| un- | il- | im- | in- | ir- |

____possible   ____necessary   ____legal   ____secure   ____regular

____adequate   ____logical   ____proper   ____believable   ____convenient

3 Change the following into words ending in **-ful**. If the word ends in a 'y', you sometimes need to change the 'y' to an 'i' before adding the suffix, but not every time!

beauty _____   grace_____   joy_____

wonder_____   bounty _____

4 Change the root words below into words with one of the following endings.

| -ian | -ion | -sion | -ssion | -tion |

electric: _____   tense: _____   complete: _____

magic: _____   confess: _____   confuse: _____

reflect: _____   permit: _____   possess: _____

5 Here is your spelling test for words with different prefixes and suffixes.

Remember to Look, Cover, Write, Check.

	1st attempt	2nd attempt	3rd attempt
autobiography			
microscope			
beautiful			
aquarium			
aeroplane			
dehydrated			
disappear			
defenceless			
transparent			
photograph			

MULTIPLE-CHOICE QUESTIONS

What you need to know

1 Learn strategies to tackle multiple-choice questions.

WINNING STRATEGIES

- At the start of your KS2 National Test Reading paper, there is always a series of **multiple-choice** questions. You don't have to write anything for these questions; you simply circle the correct answer.

- Multiple-choice questions give you a sentence about one of the texts in the reading booklet and then you are given several choices of answer. Some of the answers are quite similar to each other, to make sure you are reading carefully.

- It is really important that you go back and read each text again as you are answering the relevant questions. You can pull out the text extract section between pages 48 and 49 so you can easily refer to each text. Don't rely on your memory!

- If you make a mistake, cross out your answer and circle the correct one.

Read this short text.

> Linzy was tired of waiting. She had been in the airport for four hours now and there was still no sign of her flight. She paced up and down the departure lounge, reading the information screens; but still her flight did not appear. The sun, sea and sand of Benidorm were waiting for her; if only she could get there!

After four hours, Linzy was feeling:

(calm)   (happy)   (impatient)   (excited)

Which answer would you circle?

If you said, impatient well done – you've just earned yourself 1 mark!

- With multiple-choice questions, read both the text and the question carefully. **For example**, Linzy may well have been feeling happy and excited about going on holiday, as most of us do, but the question said after four hours. By then, Linzy was pacing up and down, so the best word to describe her feelings is: impatient. If you're not sure of an answer, it's always worth having a guess because you may be right.

Quick tips

If you read a passage and find words you don't know, try substituting the word 'something' into the passage, just to keep the flow of the sentence. Once you have read the sentence, the meaning of the unknown word may become clear. If you're still not sure, look at any pictures on the page for clues and read the sentences before and after the sentence containing the unknown word. The more of the passage you understand, the more likely you are to be able to put in a similar word which will make sense.

MULTIPLE-CHOICE QUESTIONS

1 Read Text 1. Circle the best group of words to fit the passage.

(a) Jackson was called Jackson because

| his father was called Jack. | his father may have been a sailor. | he had no mother. | he lived in Jackson Street. |

(b) This story took place

| in the autumn. | just after Christmas. | just before Christmas. | in the winter. |

(c) Paddy's Goose was

| a bird. | a person. | a street. | a building. |

(d) Jackson lived with

| his mother. | his father. | on his own. | with his family. |

2 Read Text 3. Circle the best group of words to fit the passage.

(a) When Edmund met the Queen, he was

| confused and frightened. | angry and impatient. | happy and excited. | sad and tearful. |

(b) The Queen asks Edmund if he is a 'Son of Adam'. This means

| Edmund is a dwarf. | his father is called Adam. | Edmund is human. | Edmund has a beard. |

(c) The Queen was sitting:

| on a throne. | on a horse. | in a wardrobe. | on a sledge. |

3 Read Text 5. Circle the best group of words to fit the passage.

(a) On her feet, The Match Girl was wearing

| her mother's slippers. | warm boots. | nothing. | only socks. |

(b) The Little Match Girl was scared to go home because

| she had lost her slippers. | she was cold and hungry. | it was New Year's Eve. | she hadn't sold any matches. |

(c) This story takes place

| in the evening. | in the early morning. | late at night. | at midnight. |

ORDERING AND MATCHING

What you need to know

1 Learn strategies to help you answer ordering and matching questions.

ORDERING AND MATCHING SKILLS

- For some kinds of comprehension questions you need to use ordering and matching skills. There are three main types of this kind of question:

  ordering/numbering a sequence of events; drawing a line to match two items; filling in missing information from a table or chart.

ORDERING

- You may be given a story or a set of instructions to read. This will be followed by a list of events or items and you will be asked to order them correctly. The first event will always be numbered.

  Underline the part of the text containing the first event, so that you only need to look at the text after that point for subsequent events.

  Read the text carefully, making a mental note of the order of key events. Underline any information you find.

  You may not always find exactly the same words in the text as used in the question, but it is the meaning of the words that matters.

  Look for clue words, such as first, secondly, then, and finally.

  When you have marked the order of events, read through the text again to check your answer.

MATCHING

- Some questions give you two lists of items and ask you to match them according to given criteria, for example, superheroes to their super powers.

- In order to match items it is vital to:

  read *all* the items carefully
  check the passage in the text from which the information came
  underline any relevant information
  be especially careful on questions where more than one line needs to be drawn to another item
  make sure you don't miss any item out.

- Sometimes information is presented as a table or chart with some items missing. You should:

  read through the relevant text passages
  locate the missing information and fill in the correct boxes
  always check your answers carefully.

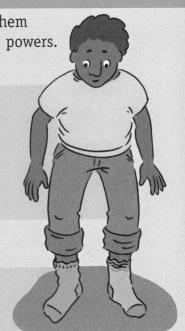

77

ORDERING AND MATCHING

1 Read Text 8: From *Liquid Magic* by Philip Watson.
Order these events in the sequence in which they occur.

At first the mothballs will sink. `1`

The mothballs lift to the surface again. ☐

Bubbles of gas collect on the mothballs. ☐

The mothballs sink to the bottom again. ☐

The mothballs dance upwards. ☐

At the surface, the gas escapes. ☐

2 Read Text 13b, the poem 'On the Ning, Nang, Ning, Nang, Nong' by Spike Milligan.
Match the creatures and objects to the sounds they make.

monkeys   clang

cows   jibber jabber joo

mice   ping

teapots   bong

trees   boo

3 Read Text 17a: from the *Island Breeze Cruises* brochure.
Fill in the missing information in the table.

Area on the ship	Activity	Time of day
Sun Deck	stretch and tone session	early morning
	musical revue	evening
Cordoba Lounge		evening
	bridge tournament	
	nightcap	late night

FINDING WORDS AND PHRASES

What you need to know

1 Learn strategies for answering 'find a word or phrase' type questions.

SEARCH STRATEGIES

- A very common type of question in the KS2 National English Test is the 'find a word or phrase' type question. These questions ask you to locate a word, phrase or a number of words or phrases on a given theme.

- It is very important to read the question and the relevant text carefully.

- Underline how many words or phrases the question is asking for.

- When you have written your answer, check it against the question to make sure you have done what the question asked.

Read this passage.

Karl and Michael were hiding in an icy cave on the edge of the beach. The waves whipped up freezing spray against their faces and their breath showed like steam in the frosty air. They huddled together and blew on their fingers. In the inky darkness at the back of the cave, they thought they saw strange shapes moving about but it was just their imaginations. Exhausted, they struggled to keep awake. Surely help would come soon!

From this passage, you might be asked a question like this:

1 Find a word that shows how tired the boys were.

Re-read the passage.

Underline any words to do with tiredness,
e.g. the sentence: **Exhausted, they struggled to keep awake.**
The best word to use in that sentence is **exhausted**
Write it down and get the mark!

I'm looking for a **word**, not a phrase.

Another question could be:

2 Find **three** words or phrases in the passage that show how cold it was in the cave.

I can use either words or phrases but I only need **three**.

You could choose from:

icy cave   frosty air   freezing spray   they huddled together
breath showed like steam   blew on their fingers

Which three would you choose?

FINDING WORDS AND PHRASES

1 Read Text 3: the extract from *The Lion, The Witch and The Wardrobe*, by C. S. Lewis.

(a) What did the Queen mean by the phrase, 'Son of Adam'?

_____

_____

(b) Find a word in the text that is similar in meaning to 'kingdoms' or 'realms'.

_____

(c) Find **two** phrases that show that Edmund was frightened and confused.

_____

_____

2 Read Text 13c: 'The Listeners' by Walter de la Mare.

(a) Find **three** words or phrases from the text, which refer to darkness.

_____

_____

_____

(b) Find a word in the text similar in meaning to 'confused'.

_____

(c) The poet writes the phrase, 'forest's ferny floor'. What is this an example of?

_____

(d) Find a word in the text similar in meaning to 'knocked'.

_____

EXPRESSING AN OPINION

What you need to know

1 Learn strategies to help you answer '3 mark' opinion type questions.

HOW MARKS ARE AWARDED

- When a KS2 Reading Test question asks for an opinion it is generally worth three marks, and therefore a detailed answer must be given.

- **No marks** are awarded for answers which could apply to any text.

- **One mark** is awarded for very general answers with trivial reasons or explanations.

- **Two marks** are given for clearly-explained answers which refer to events in the text.

- **Three marks** are awarded for answers which demonstrate insight and a clear understanding of the story and the theme of the text, and which express reasoned, critical opinions.

TACKLING OPINION TYPE QUESTIONS

- Here are some possible answers to the following question about a mystery story.

> **1** Did you enjoy the story?
> Explain your views as fully as you can.

Remember
For '3 mark' opinion type questions, you must write detailed answers, preferably in complete sentences. Think before you write, and read your answer again to check it makes sense.

Only **one mark** would be given for these type of answers:

> *Yes, I enjoyed the story because it was mysterious.   It had nice descriptions.*
> *I liked the story because it was exciting/interesting.   I liked the characters.*

The writer has made a relevant comment about the text, but has not added any detail, or referred to anything that happened that was mysterious.

Two marks would be given for an answer with a little more detail and reference to something that happened in the text, or some dialogue spoken by a character.

> *It was mysterious when the light went off without anyone touching it.*

Three marks would be given for a well-thought out, detailed answer, that refers to events in the text and shows a good understanding of the story and the characters' actions.

> *I thought the story was mysterious, because a lot of unexplained things happened, such as the light going off without anyone touching it, the wind blowing the papers around the desk and the door slamming shut. I would have been frightened if I was in that house, so I think that the two children showed bravery by staying there for the whole night and saying 'Nothing is going to scare me away'.*

EXPRESSING AN OPINION

1   Read Text 5: the extract from *The Little Match Girl*, by Hans Christian Andersen.

(a)   Did you enjoy reading the extract about The Little Match Girl?   **Yes**   **No**
Give reasons for your answer, referring to the text.

_____

_____

_____

_____

(b)   What do you think The Little Match Girl will do next in the story?
Give reasons for your answer.

_____

_____

_____

_____

2   Read Text 19: 'A Changing World' from *The Blue Peter Green Book*.

(a) In your opinion, from reading the text, why should we save the rainforests?

_____

_____

_____

_____

(b)   Is this article effective in describing the effects of global warming?

Yes   **No**

Explain your answer with reference to the text.

_____

_____

_____

_____

COMPARING AND CONTRASTING TEXTS

What you need to know

1 Be able to compare and contrast two or more texts.

COMPARE AND CONTRAST QUESTIONS

- 'Compare and contrast' questions ask you to look at two or more texts and to write about each of them, saying what is similar about them and what is different.

  You might be asked to compare poems on a similar theme, or story openings.

  In non-chronological writing, you might be asked to compare two newspaper reports or letters.

  You might be asked whether the authors have been effective in putting forward their message or creating an atmosphere.

  You might be asked about the language used in the texts, whether the texts are biased or objective, or which of the texts you prefer.

- These type of questions are often worth three marks, so your answers need to be very detailed.

HOW TO ANSWER

- To answer compare and contrast questions effectively:

  read the relevant texts again,

  underline any words or phrases you might use or that you will refer to in your answer,

  write down your comparison, referring to both texts.

  If you only talk about one text, you won't get all your marks.

- Here is a sample answer based on Text 3 (the excerpt from *The Lion, The Witch and The Wardrobe*, by C. S. Lewis) and Text 5 (*The Little Match Girl*, by Hans Christian Andersen).

  > **1** Which passage do you think is more effective in creating a sense of character?

  I think that Text 3 is more effective in creating a sense of character through the use of dialogue to show how a character behaves and thinks. In The Little Match Girl, we learn a lot about how the main character feels, but more about the coldness of the night in the city. In The Lion, the Witch and the Wardrobe text, we get a good sense of the Queen's scheming character from the way she shouts impatiently at Edmund and then changes her voice when she realises he could be useful to her.

  This answer is very detailed, and would get three marks. You will not find these answers written down in the text; you have to 'read between the lines' and think about the effect the words have on the reader.

Remember
Always, check your answer by reading it again!

COMPARING AND CONTRASTING TEXTS

1 Read Text 6a and 6b: the letter to the Editor of the Langfield Echo and the Editor's letter to the readers.

(a) Compare the two letters, saying which one is written more objectively. Give reasons for your answer.

_____

_____

_____

_____

(b) Of the two letters, which do you think is the more successful at making people aware of the dangers of illegal parking and why?

_____

_____

_____

_____

_____

2 Read Texts 18a and b: the two articles about a football match.

(a) Which of the two newspaper reports did you enjoy reading more? Give reasons for your answer.

_____

_____

_____

_____

(b) Of the two reports, which do you think captures the atmosphere of the game better? Give examples from the text to support your answer.

_____

_____

_____

KS2 PRACTICE READING TEST

Questions about Text 20 'Cookie Snatchers!'

Choose the best group of words to fit the passage.
Circle your choice.

1 The robbery had taken place

in the morning.   at lunchtime.   in the afternoon.   during the night.

1 mark

2 The thieves

got in through   lived in the   came through   forced the
a window.   house.   the garden.   door open.

1 mark

3 Mrs Llewellyn worked

in a garden.   in a school.   in an office   in a kitchen.
                                   in her house.

1 mark

4 The cookies had disappeared while

she was paying   Mrs Llewellyn   she was in   she was
the milkman.   was working.   the kitchen.   cleaning up.

1 mark

5 Mrs Llewellyn said she was 'houseproud'. This means

she was proud   she liked everything   she worked   she didn't like
of her house.   clean and tidy.   hard.   cleaning.

1 mark

6 Why had Mrs Llewellyn put the cookies on top of the cupboard?

_____

_____

2 marks

7 Find and write down **two** reasons why the detective thought that the theft must be an 'inside job'.

_____

_____

2 marks

8 Write down **three** clues that the detective spotted in the kitchen.

(i) _____

(ii) _____

(iii) _____

3 marks

9 The text says: 'his efforts... were vaguely hampered by Scruff.'
What is the meaning of the word 'hampered' in this situation?

_____

_____

2 marks

10 Did you enjoy reading this story?

Yes   **No**

Explain your reasons as fully as possible.
Refer to examples in the text to back up your opinions.

_____

_____

_____

_____

3 marks

Questions about Text 21 'Famous Literary Detectives and their Authors'

11 Fill in the following chart with information from the text, 'Famous Literary Detectives and their Authors'.

Character	Assistant	Author
Sherlock Holmes		Sir Arthur Conan Doyle
	Hastings	Agatha Christie
	Bunter	
		Colin Dexter
Lord Peter Wimsey		

4 marks

12 Why do you think the writing in this section is set out in boxes?

_____

_____

2 marks

13 Why are the names of the authors and characters in bold?

_____

_____

1 mark

14 Who was Montague Egg?

_____

_____

1 mark

15 How did Sherlock Holmes get his name?

_____

_____

1 mark

16 In this section, which author is the only one still alive?

_____

1 mark

17 Choose **two** detectives and write down **two** things they are famous for.

Name of detective: Famous for:

(i)   _____   _____   _____

(ii)   _____   _____   _____

4 marks

18 Hercule Poirot uses his 'little grey cells' to solve cases.
What do you think is meant by this phrase?

_____

_____

2 marks

19 How did Agatha Christie cause a mystery of her own?

_____

_____

1 mark

20 Why does Miss Marple seem unlike the average detective?

_____

_____

_____

2 marks

Questions about Text 22 'Becoming a Reading Detective'

21 The best term to describe this piece of writing is:

a letter   a conversation   an interview   a play

1 mark

22 What does Claire Roberts mean by the expression 'reading detective'?

_____

_____

2 marks

23 Find and write down **three** ways that being a reading detective is like being a real detective.

(i) _____

(ii) _____

(iii) _____

3 marks

24 Write down a word or phrase similar in meaning to the following words taken from the text:

(i) national _____

(ii) variety _____

(iii) inspire _____

3 marks

25 Why does Claire Roberts think that books are not the only way to improve your reading skills?

_____

_____

_____

2 marks

Questions about all the texts

26 Which of the three texts did you most enjoy reading?

Explain your reasons as fully as you can.

_____

_____

_____

_____

3 marks

KS2 PRACTICE WRITING TEST

Longer Writing Task

You have **45 minutes** in which to plan and write this piece of writing. Aim to spend about **10 minutes** on your planning and the rest of the time on your writing. Leave yourself enough time at the end of the task to check your work.

> *The boy in the bright, green coat was waving frantically at me from across the road. I had never seen him before in my life. Panting, he handed me a parcel and said, "You'll know what to do!" Then he seemed to vanish as quickly as he had appeared, leaving me stunned on the pavement.*

Continue this story. Think about:
- the characters involved
- the setting(s)
- using dialogue to move the story on
- the problems and resolutions you will write
- the action that will happen
- a satisfying ending.

Shorter Writing Task

You have **20 minutes** to complete this piece of writing, including planning time. Try to spend about **5 minutes** on your planning and **15 minutes** on your writing. Leave yourself enough time at the end of the task to check your work.

> *The local school held its Summer Fayre last Friday. Everything was going well; there were lots of stalls, raffles and games and people were enjoying themselves. Then, one of the teachers noticed that the main raffle prize of a portable television had disappeared! The police were called and an investigation followed.*

Imagine that you are a newspaper reporter who has been asked to cover this story. Your task is to write a newspaper report about the incident.

Think about:
- a suitable headline
- the date, time and place the incident happened
- what happened
- who was involved
- witness statements
- statements from the police
- was the case solved?

KS2 PRACTICE SPELLING TEST

Ask an adult to read the Practice Spelling Test aloud to you twice. During the first reading, follow the text, but don't write anything. During the second reading, try to spell the words which fit in the blank spaces. There are 20 spellings in this test.

It was _____ now. All the _____ ☐ ☐

had left the market and the sun had left the sky. Stalls had been

_____ and the market traders had gone home to ☐

count the day's takings. Philip and Rachael felt safe _____ ☐

to emerge from the shadows.

_____ , a noise startled them. The sound of an engine ☐

roared and a _____ red dustcart came to take away ☐

all the _____ boxes and unsold fruit. Rachael grabbed ☐

a handful of _____ without being seen. The dustcart ☐

roared again and _____ over the cobbles, rattling as ☐

it passed _____ . ☐

"I'm _____ !" whispered Rachael. ☐

"We both are!" Philip agreed. "But we can't give up now. We must keep

_____ ." ☐

"But where will we go, Philip? Where will we sleep?" She sucked her

_____ anxiously. ☐

"I don't _____ , Rachael," he said warmly to his younger ☐

sister. "But we can't stay here. Everything's _____ now." ☐

Philip did not let on how _____ ☐

the situation had become. Rachael was too young to

understand, but he wasn't about to let the two of

them get _____ . Their ☐

mother wasn't _____ ☐

of being a spy; no matter what anyone said, and

they would find the evidence to prove her

_____ , even if they had ☐

to walk to the ends of the _____ . ☐

Note to parents
You will find the complete text for this Spelling Test on page 4. Read your version through once to your child, then on the second read, pause after each underlined word so they can fill in the words on this page.

ASSESSING YOUR CHILD'S WRITING

From 2003, the way in which children's writing is assessed in the National Tests has changed. The marking criteria are now specific to the task set and are not level specific. This section includes a way of assessing writing so that an approximate level can be given.

For the longer task, there is a maximum of 28 marks, awarded for sentence structure and punctuation, text structure and organization, and composition and effect. The shorter task carries a possible 12 marks, with sentence structure, punctuation and text organization assessed together and composition and effect being the other component.

To assess your child's work, look at their writing for the following qualities and components, and award marks up to the maximum shown. If your child does not meet the criteria for maximum marks in each section, parental judgement must be exercised to award a reasonable number of marks, based on how far from the ideal their writing is.

Longer Task
Sentence structure and organization (maximum 8 marks)
- Sentences of varying lengths, written with clarity, purpose and effect.
- Accuracy of syntax and punctuation in sentences, clauses and phrases.

Text structure and organization (maximum 8 marks)
- Whole texts are presented effectively, with information, events and ideas sequenced and structured logically.
- Writing is divided into paragraphs which follow on from each other and are appropriate divisions of the text.

Composition and effect (maximum 12 marks)
- Children are able to write imaginative, interesting and thoughtful texts with good use of language, including adjectives, adverbs, etc.
- Texts are appropriate to purpose and to the reader for whom they were intended.

Shorter Task
Sentence structure, punctuation and text organization (maximum 4 marks)
- Sentences of varying lengths, written with clarity, purpose and effect.
- Accuracy of syntax and punctuation in sentences, clauses and phrases.
- Writing is divided into paragraphs which follow on from each other and are appropriate divisions of the text.

Composition and effect (maximum 8 marks)
- Children are able to write imaginative, interesting and thoughtful texts with good use of language, including adjectives, adverbs, etc.
- Texts are appropriate to purpose and to the reader for whom they are intended.

A more detailed marking system, explaining the changes more fully, can be obtained from the QCA website: www.qca.org.uk/ca/tests/2003sample.

Awarding a level
Once you have added up all the comprehension marks for the Practice Test (maximum 50 marks) and have made an assessment of your child's writing for the longer and shorter task, there are two more areas to assess before an approximate level can be awarded.

Spelling
The spelling test is marked out of 20, but from 2003 a maximum of seven marks will be awarded. The marks will be aggregated to a scale of one to seven marks, along these lines:

18 to 20 correct	-	7 marks
16 to 17 correct	-	6 marks
14 to 15 correct	-	5 marks
12 to 13 correct	-	4 marks
10 to 11 correct	-	3 marks
8 to 9 correct	-	2 marks
5 to 7 correct	-	1 mark
below 5	-	no marks

Handwriting
Handwriting is no longer assessed separately. To assess your child's handwriting, choose a few sentences from one of the longer writing tasks, where their best writing appears.

Handwriting now carries a maximum of three marks.
1 mark: Handwriting is legible and shows some regularity of size and spacing. Overall, however, the writing is uneven and disjointed.
2 marks: The handwriting is regular with some flow and movement. There is some variation in size, but letters and words are usually appropriate in size and position.
3 marks: Handwriting is consistent and fluent with letters and words appropriately placed. There is evidence of a personal style, usually joined, which engages the reader. Handwriting is clear and letters well-formed.

Once all these assessments have been made and a score out of 100 marks arrived at, an approximate level can be awarded. It is difficult to be precise about the exact marks which constitute a particular level as each year the thresholds for a level change by two or three marks up or down, according to national achievement. Therefore these marks and levels are to be used only as a guide.

78 to 80+ marks - expected Level 5
48 to 52 marks up to 78 to 80 marks - expected Level 4
28 marks up to 48 to 52 marks - expected Level 3
Below 28 marks - expected Level 2 or below.

Children who achieve below 25 marks may not be entered for their English National Test paper, but be assessed by the teacher, who awards a Level 2 on their behalf.

Once you have assessed your child's strengths and weaknesses, you will know the areas for development and more practice in these areas can be carried out.

ANSWERS TO ACTIVITIES FOR WEEKS 1-8

Sentences and parts of speech Week 1 Monday
1 (a) Oh no! I'm late! **(b)** Where are you supposed to be, Simon?
(c) On my way to the football match. **(d)** What time does the match start? **(e)** Kick off is at three o'clock. Where is my scarf, Helen?
(f) For goodness sake, it's in the drawer where it always is!
(g) I can't find it. Can you help me? **(h)** Here it is!
2 (a) I went on a cruise last year and visited: Crete, Cyprus, Malta and Majorca. **(b)** Of all the books in the library, my favourite is Jane Eyre by Charlotte Bronte. **(c)** On Monday, I was surprised to see a frog sitting at the end of my bed. **(d)** The supermarket in the High Street is giving away balloons with every purchase.
3 (a) He was struggling with his homework *or* He was struggling with it. **(b)** She had no time to play. **(c)** His football had a hole in it. He would have to blow it up again.

Commas and colons Week 1 Tuesday
1 (a) Susie decided to invite Julie, Carrie, Jane and Sarah to her party.
(b) John prepared a meal of cold meats, potatoes, salad and bread.
(c) The cat leapt out of the window, ran along the path then hid under the car. **(d)** Ivy told me she lived at 5, Briar Road, Newtown, Yorkshire. **(e)** The cold, wet, windy weather made Simon miserable.
2 (a) Omar's school bag contained many things: books, pencils, pens and sweets. **(b)** The witch put in her cauldron: mice, serpent's skin, school custard and tapioca. **(c)** Gary gave the teacher his home address: 12 Lilac Gardens, Oldwood. **(d)** Anne did not realize how late it was: she had lost track of the time. **(e)** Ali was unsure of where to go: he was lost in the maze.
3 (a) Helen, trying not to laugh, admired her sister's new haircut.
(b) Mr. Fenwick, who was making everyone a cup of tea, was unaware of the argument brewing in his living room. **(c)** Mina, listening carefully, wrote down the instructions. **(d)** Scott, at the back of the class, had fallen off his chair. **(e)** The netball player, having just joined the team, was very nervous.

Speech marks Week 1 Wednesday
1 (a) The guitarist complained, "My string has snapped again!"
(b) The crowd shouted, "More! More!" **(c)** "Who can find Australia on a map?" asked the teacher. **(d)** "Are we nearly there yet?" whinged the children in the back of the car. **(e)** "It was my fault," admitted the pupil, "I broke the ruler."
2 (a) whispered **(b)** demanded **(c)** shrieked **(d)** stuttered **(e)** cried
3 (a) Karl shouted that he was off to the match. **(b)** Abbi said that she had had a lovely time in Florida. **(c)** Liam replied that his school report was really good this year.

Paragraphs Week 1 Thursday
1 Paragraph 1: Description of Jackson. Paragraph 2: How he got his name. Paragraph 3: When Jackson went missing.
2 Jenny Pigtails
Jenny Pigtails they called her, because of her long, red plaits. "Jenny Pigtails!" they would shout, and run away, laughing. But Jenny wasn't bothered by their names. She had more important things to worry about, and anyway, she liked her red, unruly hair. Plaiting it was the only way to keep it in check; otherwise it fell round her shoulders like a huge cape.
The school bell sounded and Jenny lined up with the others. She stood behind her friend, Emily Souter, and they chatted about nothing much until the teacher came out to the line. Jenny liked Mrs. Walton, who always smiled at her and helped her to do her work. When it was their turn, Class 5 marched in.
Inside, Jenny could smell antiseptic, and in a small room off the hall, she caught sight of the school nurse. Oh no, today was the day for Class 5's TB injections and Jenny was terrified of needles!
3 *Check that your child has written in paragraphs with an indent at the start of each new paragraph and has covered the points in the question.*

Spelling: double consonants Week 1 Friday
1 (a) bubbles, bottle, fizzing, effect **(b)** sunny, humming, buzzing
(c) fluffy, pillows, better
2 (a) puddle **(b)** mirror **(c)** wrapper **(d)** letter **(e)** missing
3 ladder butter luggage suddenly lesson
4 *This spelling test can be given more than once to check that your child has remembered the various spelling rules.*

Adjectives and adverbs Week 2 Monday
1 and **2 (a)** to **(e)** *Check that your child has completed each sentence with appropriate adjectives/adverbs. Part of the purpose of this activity is to make children realize how many different adjectives and adverbs are at their disposal and to practise using a thesaurus.*

3 (a) More than ever, she wanted to win the competition. **(b)** The feathers fell, like crystal snowflakes, from the burst pillow. **(c)** In a loud voice, the child shouted across the valley. **(d)** The old clock had stood, at the far end of the street, for many years. **(e)** The mice crept across the floor, as quietly as they could.

Characters Week 2 Tuesday
1 Graham was the youngest in his family, although he **looked a lot older than** his 25 years. His face was **dirty and crumpled like an old paper bag**. His small, beady eyes were nut-brown and made **sharp points on his face**. He rarely smiled; he had nothing to smile about. Hands **thrust into bottomless pockets**, he trudged through the early morning streets towards the factory. Another hard day, he thought to himself.
2 *In your child's answer, look for detail of description; use of adjectives; clarity and description of personality/character as well as external features.*

Setting the scene Week 2 Wednesday
1 *Make sure that the descriptions used match the relevant senses.*
2 *Accept any appropriate words and phrases. If your child needs further practice, you could write other description frames in other settings for your child to fill in.*

Story planning Week 2 Thursday
1 *Make sure that one story start begins with action, one with dialogue and one with description. If your child has particular difficulty with one aspect, look through some novels or short stories to see how they start and to give them a bank of ideas.*
2 *Check that your child has:* • started well • included interesting characters • described people and places • written in paragraphs • included some dialogue • included problems and resolutions • ended the story well. *Look to see what your child has done well and build on that. Reinforce weaker areas through more practice.*

Spelling: modifying 'e' Week 2 Friday
1 hope, spite, scare, cure, Pete. *Accept any sentence in which the given word has been used appropriately.*
2 (a) pavement **(b)** telephone **(c)** hotel, lonely **(d)** advice, exercise **(e)** continue, refuse, home.
3 *This spelling test can be given more than once to check that your child has remembered the various spelling rules.*

Letter writing Week 3 Monday
1 (a) Mrs. Barras is hoping that her letter will be published in the newspaper in order to draw attention to her problem. She hopes that drivers will read her letter and stop parking near the school. She is hoping that other parents will read her letter and start walking to school. The newspaper is already looking at the dangers of parking outside city schools, so she hopes that her letter will be included in their campaign. **(b)** The parked cars are blocking the road so that people with prams can't get past; the cars are stopping people from seeing what is coming when they cross the road because they are blocking the road. **(c)** The editor of the local paper wants to attract people to the public meeting so that they can put their views forward to the police, the councillors, the road safety department and the MP who will be there. The paper is concerned about parking outside city schools and wants people to do something about it.
2 (a) *Possible answers are:* Text 7a is an informal letter, whereas Text 7b is a more formal letter. Text 7a is a happy letter about getting a new dog, but Text 7b is an angry letter about dogs. Text 7a wants to take the dog to the lake to go in the water but Text 7b wants to stop dog owners from letting dogs off the leash near the lake. Text 7a is to a friend but Text 7b is to the Environmental Health Department. *Children may find other differences.*
(b) *Look for any appropriate response, backed up by reference to the text.* Generally, your child's answer should reflect the feeling that Jonathon will be happy and possibly excited when he receives his letter as it is from a friend and he is being invited to stay at his friend's house. However, Mr. Nettleworth may feel concerned or even angry that the council signs are being ignored and feel that he needs to do something about the problem.

Formal and informal letters Week 3 Tuesday
1, 2 and **3** *For each activity:* check that your child's letter is correctly set out with the address and date; has relevant ideas presented clearly and, if possible, is organized into paragraphs; and has an appropriate ending.

Instructions Week 3 Wednesday
1 2 Secondly, take the kettle and fill it with water. 7 Finally, stir it well, sit back and enjoy it. 3 After filling the kettle, switch it on.

4 While you are waiting for the kettle to boil, put a spoonful of coffee in a cup or mug and if you like, a spoonful or two of sugar. 6 Once you have poured in the water, add a little milk. 1 First you need a kettle, a cup or mug and a spoon. 5 When the kettle has boiled, pour water in the cup until it is almost full.

2 (a) The writer lists the materials first so you know what you will need to get ready before you start. (b) *Choose from:* put, read, clear, take, never, clean, wash, colour, add, drop. (c) *Possible answers are:* Imperative words are clear. They are orders. It is telling you what to do. They are simple words that tell you what to do.

3 *The instruction should include a valid reason for the choice, e.g.* I would choose never eat or drink anything unless told you may do. I have chosen this because you could be ill if you eat or drink something from an experiment. It might be poisonous or dangerous to do that.

4 'Dance' means float up to the surface and bob up and down a bit, like a dancer.

Analysing instructions   Week 3 Thursday

1 1 Firstly, find the tree with the cracked trunk and stand to the North side of it. 2 Secondly, walk three large steps in a westerly direction and stop. 3 The third thing you must do is make a quarter turn to the left and walk ten paces; you should stop just in front of an oddly-shaped and very heavy rock. 4 After coming to the rock, look up; you should see an overhanging branch which will point in the direction you now should go. 5 Once you have spotted the branch, walk six paces in the direction it is pointing and stop. 6 Finally, make sure no-one is looking and dig! The treasure is buried 30 cm below ground level and is wrapped in a plastic bag.

2 *Accept any reasonable answers.*

3 *Possible answers:* make you very rich; an enormous amount of very valuable Roman coins; you will be wealthy beyond your wildest dreams; treasure; you will not believe how much they are worth; you will be well rewarded.

4 *Check that you can follow your child's instructions clearly.*

Spelling: silent letters   Week 3 Friday

1 (a) wrist (b) listen (c) Which (d) knight (e) hours (f) Science (g) crumbs

2 *2 across* scent *4 across* whistle *6 across* crumb
1 down gnat *2 down* scheme *3 down* design *5 down* limb

3 *This spelling test can be given more than once to check that your child has remembered the various spelling rules.*

Similes, metaphors and personification   Week 4 Monday

1 (a) His marks are honeycomb. His back patterns are stars in the moonlight. (b) His eyes are like flying saucers. His ribs stretch like elastic bands (c) *Accept any appropriate simile.*

2 *This is quite hard, so you may like to help in the planning of this poem. Ensure that your child's finished poem meets the given criteria of three simile and two metaphors.*

3 (a) In this case, 'exact' means 'precise, truthful', as the mirror reflects the true image of the onlooker. (b) see, swallow (c) This is similar in meaning to the first line. The mirror reflects back only what is there. It is not making the image any worse, just showing the image as it really is.

4 *Check that the poem contains verbs giving the object human qualities or feelings.*

Alliteration, assonance and onomatopoeia   Week 4 Tuesday

1 (a) *Choose from:* silver sparkles, sit and stare, frilly fish, tiny tadpoles. (b) 'green-backed croakers' are frogs (c) 'silver sparkles' are the reflections of sunlight on the water

2 (a) *Choose combinations from:* hairy, scary, wary, contrary; highly wily, slyly smiley. (b) The message is to follow your instincts and don't be taken in by appearances alone.

3 Seven onomatopoeic words: bang, clatter, squelch, splash, crack, rustle, crunch.

4 (a) splash (b) buzzing (c) snap (d) zoomed (e) swishing

Exploring different forms of poetry (1)   Week 4 Wednesday

1 *Reinforce the notion of syllables if this seems to be causing difficulties. Check that your child's Haiku follows the format: 5 syllables, 7 syllables, 5 syllables.*

2 *Check that your child's kenning follows the rules (see page 39) and has appropriate describing words for the chosen animal.*

3 *This form of poetry is probably the hardest of all three to write, so help should be offered. Your child's poem should follow the Tanka form with 5, 7, 5, 7, 7 syllables.*

Exploring differnt forms of poetry (2)   Week 4 Thursday

1 (a) The person sat in a front seat at the back. (b) You can't fall from the pit to the gallery, because the pit is on the ground and the gallery is one of the high tiers of seating in a theatre. You can't fall up. (c) *Choose from:* went to the pictures tomorrow, broke a front bone in my back; ate chocolate and gave it back.

2 (a) *Choose from:* Ning Nang Nong; Nong, Nang Ning; Nong, Ning, Nang; Jibber Jabber Joo (b) *Choose from:* cows go bong!; trees go ping!; mice go clang! (c) *Choose from:* monkeys can't talk so they couldn't say Boo; trees don't go Ping; teapots can't Jibber Jabber Joo; mice don't go Clang.

3 (a) The Traveller has arrived at a building in a forest. It might be a castle or large house, because it mentions a turret. (b) The Listeners are the ghosts or spirits of the people who used to live in the building. (c) The poem takes place at night. Phrases that tell us this are: moonlit door; in the quiet of the moonlight; thronging the faint moonbeams; dark stair; dark turf; starred and leafy sky. (d) The Traveller had come to the building to keep a promise he had made long ago. 'Tell them I came, and no one answered, That I kept my word', he said.

Spelling: soft c and g   Week 4 Friday

1 cymbal, sentence, cylinder, ceiling, dancing

2 gentle, gymnast, giant, rage, germ

3 A genius gymnast from Slough,
Made a giant leap over a cow.
This graceful athlete
Was so light on his feet
That the crowd gave a gigantic WOW!

4 *This spelling test can be given more than once to check that your child has remembered the various spelling rules.*

Analysing playscripts   Week 5 Monday

1 (a) The narrator sets the scene and explains what has happened before the play starts. The narrator also introduces some of the main characters. (b) ambush him as he walked in his garden; 'accidentally' fall into the River Nile. (c) immortal – will live for ever; undying; can't be killed (*or similar*) (d) Osiris must give his life up willingly if Set is to become ruler of Egypt.

2 *The answer should be supported by examples from the text, e.g.* (a) Cai seems to be impatient, he says, "No time to stop. I tell you. My time is short enough.". He is concerned about finding a good place for his family to settle and takes their feelings into account, he says "I see this field is good for you, Morgan." He is religious, he suggests asking God to bless the earth where they have chosen to stay. (b) The hills look misty because they are now in the distance and can't be easily made out. They could also be misty because their tops may be in the clouds. (c) *Choose two from:* the mountains give shelter from the cold; there's food on the berry bushes; there is a rich valley in which to grow crops; there are stones to build houses with and there is water to drink.

Writing playscripts   Week 5 Tuesday

1 *Here is one possible version of the conversation. Accept any suitable alternative stage directions.* Scene 1: Morven and Steven are preparing to go on holiday. Morven is excited.

Morven: (anxiously) Have we got everything we need, Steven? What about the first aid kit?
Steven: (reassuringly) Don't worry. I've checked everything twice.
Mum: (entering the room and looking worried) Have you got your passports, because you won't get very far without those! (Dad enters through the front door. He seems impatient)
Dad: (gruffly) Isn't anyone coming? I've had the engine running for five minutes. Don't you want to catch that plane?
Morven: (rushing to collect her bags) Come on. Let's go!

2 *The short playscript should show the conventions learnt in this unit. Check that the words the characters say are appropriate and that directions have been given. Make sure that the words are set out in the form of a playscript.*

3 *This activity is similar to that above, except this one draws on real life and therefore should be easier for your child to come up with a storyline. Check that the work is written in the form of a playscript.*

Analysing interviews   Week 5 Wednesday

1 (a) The writing is set out this way to show it is an interview. The names on the left before each new piece tell us who is speaking. (b) He started twenty-five years ago. (c) Closed, although the interviewee was able to expand his answer a little. (d) *Choose from:* What made you want to become a songwriter? How do you decide on an idea for a song? What advice can you give to young

song-writers? **(e)** From things that have happened to him, or people he has met or things he has seen in the news.

2 *Accept appropriate open questions. Examples could be:*
(i) Can you tell me about your greatest songwriting achievement?
(ii) What would you still like to achieve through your songwriting?
(iii) Is there anything in your life that has particularly influenced your songwriting?

3 'tinkering' means playing around, trying out things, trying different combinations or ideas.

4 Jim took ten minutes to write some songs and two years for others. Some he has started but not finished, so he can't say how long a song will take.

Writing interviews   Week 5 Thursday
1 **(a)** closed **(b)** open **(c)** open **(d)** closed **(e)** open
2 *Answer suggestions:* **(a)** What can you tell me about your childhood? **(b)** What can you tell me about the books you have written? **(c)** Tell me about your next book and what it is to be called? **(d)** Could you describe how your last idea came to you? **(e)** What are the good points and bad points about being a writer?
3 and 4 *Encourage your child to practise their interviewing skills. Help them to formulate questions and take on the part of the interviewee. Then check that your child has written in interview form and has included a range of relevant questions with open and closed questions.*

Spelling: plurals   Week 5 Friday
1 monkey – monkeys; house – houses; party – parties; scarf – scarves (*or* scarfs); valley – valleys; wolf – wolves; crash – crashes; baby – babies; half – halves; elephant – elephants
2 child – children; woman – women; person – people (*persons is archaic but technically acceptable*); sheep – sheep; mouse – mice; man – men.
3 *This spelling test can be given more than once to check that your child has remembered the various spelling rules.*

Analysing persuasive writing   Week 6 Monday
1 **(a)** Mrs. Barrass is complaining about parked cars near her children's school. She is worried about children getting knocked over. **(b)** *Choose from:* there have been hundreds of accidents near the school; it is only a matter of time until someone is killed; all the drivers are mad; all the parents agree with her. **(c)** walk to school instead of taking the car; stop motorists parking on the zig-zag lines (i.e. too near the school) **(d)** ever-present – always there; vulnerable – open to danger, able to be hurt, sensitive; obscuring – covering up, getting in the way of, hiding
2 **(a)** *Choose from:* it is small; lightweight; hand-held; searches for answers to homework questions; contains over five million facts; linked to the National Curriculum; it has finger-friendly keys; Internet compatible; has an amazing memory. **(b)** *Choose from answers similar to:* the advertisers tell you 'don't worry any longer'; it is the answer to all your problems; it is only £149.99; its cutting edge technology can save you time and tears; it says that it can solve all your homework problems; it says it can find answers quicker than you can ask your parents; it is always ready to help, unlike your parents; it seems easy to use. **(c)** The advertisement is aimed at children of about 10 to 16 who have a lot of homework and get stuck/need help. **(d)** *Supporting evidence:* the text mentions homework; the National Curriculum; asking your parents; it mentions school subjects like history and maths; all of which back up the theory that it is designed for children.

Writing persuasively   Week 6 Tuesday
1 *Make sure your child has:* followed the letter writing format, mentioned all the relevant points listed and has used persuasive language to convince people to adopt their thinking. *Encourage your child to start a new paragraph for each new point, if possible.*
2 *Look for a well-designed poster that is aimed at getting young children to eat more healthily. A quick check list for the poster/advertisement would be:* • is there a snappy slogan(s)? • is the message clear? • has persuasive language been used? • is the information relevant? • will it appeal to its target audience?

Analysing leaflets   Week 6 Wednesday
1 **(a)** The passengers receive a copy of the Cruises News each day. **(b)** *Accept your child's personal choice with a relevant reason.* **(c)** *Choose from:* stretch and tone on the Sun Deck; learn to line dance; go to the ship's gym; bridge tournament; bingo; name that tune; learn to mix cocktails.
2 **(a)** To inform people about the new water park opening and to persuade people to use it. **(b)** 10:00 a.m. to 5:00 p.m. **(c)** She was

chosen because she has a new record to promote and it is called 'Splash' which fits in with the theme of the water park. People may come just to see her if they like her record. **(d)** *Choose from:* spa bath; 3 flumes (slides); jacuzzi; surfing pool with bodyboards; Poolside Bistro **(e)** £1.50 **(f)** The writer is daring the reader to try the ride, which suggests it might be scary or exciting. This is to persuade people to have a go, by making it sound as if only the bravest people would dare to try it. **(g)** *Your child's choice of activities should be accompanied by relevant reasons.*

Leaflets and brochures   Week 6 Thursday
1 and 2 *The answers to both these questions need to be quite detailed and will rely on your child's imagination as well as their use of persuasive writing. Make sure that your child has included all or most of the relevant information requested and has presented it in an interesting and/or clear way.*

Spelling: vowel diagraphs   Week 6 Friday
1 friend, ceiling, neither, thief, field, niece, receipt, deceive, priest, chief.
2 thread, applaud, Autumn, neighbours, wound, penguin, captain, avoid, potatoes.
3 Wordsearch: echoes, couple, unchain, belief, haul, vault, eight, moisture, cocoa, juice, waist, believe, reign, height, roast.
4 *This spelling test can be given more than once to check that your child has remembered the various spelling rules.*

Newspaper reports   Week 7 Monday
1 **(a)** Grangetown Wanderers 4, Herrington Rovers 1 **(b)** George Fenwick scored four for Grangetown, Watson scored one goal for Herrington. **(c)** Just before half time **(d)** This is an important season for George Fenwick as he has just announced his retirement, so this is his last season as a professional footballer. **(e)** The Grangetown left back is called Gary Loadman. **(f)** The Herrington goalkeeper has just returned after a back injury and is not yet back to full fitness.
2 Using emotional words builds up the excitement for the reader, so they can imagine what it must have been like to be there. Words like 'screaming shot' tell us how fast the ball was going and 'fever pitch' tells us how excited the crowd were. The words chosen are more exciting than 'kicked', 'scored a goal' and give atmosphere to the event.
3 stellar – star like, brilliant, shining; adversary – opponent; consolation – to make them feel better, comforting
4 **(a)** Your child's choice should be backed up with reasons. **(b)** *Look for appropriate titles in newspaper format.*

Writing a newspaper report   Week 7 Tuesday
1 **(a)** Each title should read like a newspaper headline and be relevant to the article for which it was intended. **(b)** This activity allows your child to extend their skills, by thinking up a headline and starting to write the article in newspaper form.
2 and 3 *Encourage your child to plan out their articles using the planning frame on page 67. Each completed article should show features of journalistic writing.*

Bias   Week 7 Wednesday
1 **(a)** This extract is about someone's opinion based on facts. **(b)** The writer has used subheadings to organize the information into clearer sections; you know what he will be writing about in each section. **(c)** The writer uses the term 'Aladdin's Cave' to describe the rainforests because Aladdin's cave was full of jewels and gold and the writer thinks that the rainforests are full of riches of a different kind, but they are still precious. Also the bright colours of the rainforest and its animals may make the writer think of jewels. **(d)** The writer has used these words in inverted commas because he doesn't really think we are civilised. He uses the word 'develop' because he thinks that rather than develop the rainforests, people want to pull them down and destroy them.
2 **(a)** pollution; people **(b)** *Accept any three, appropriate adjectives.* **(c)** *Accept answers similar to:* The writer has made me feel worried, because he says that dolphins are in danger and I like dolphins. I am worried that more and more will get caught in tuna fishermen's nets and they might die out. I do not like the thought of them drowning.
3 **(a)** *Choose from:* the Arctic will become warmer by about 8°C; the Arctic region ice may break up; sea levels will rise; vast areas will be flooded. **(b)** *Answers will be similar to:* The author believes that the world is in danger if people don't stop and think about what is happening. We might lose the rainforests and with it, cures for illnesses and plants that could make medicines. We might lose dolphins if we don't stop polluting the water and make fishermen take more care. Lastly, through global warming, we could see floods and the melting of the Arctic ice. This would all be terrible for our planet and we must try and stop it.

Writing a balanced argument — Week 7 Thursday

1 *The writing should be in report form, written objectively and cover the main points suggested in the activity prompt. This activity should be fairly straightforward for your child, especially if they have owned a pet before, as they can write from experience.*

2 *This activity is more difficult as it is a balanced argument and children find this quite tricky. Encourage your child to plan the points for and against their argument first and then to organize them into paragraphs. The subject matter is within their grasp and they are sure to have an opinion of their own about this subject. However, the skill here is to put both sides of the argument.*

Spelling: prefixes and suffixes — Week 7 Friday

1 (a) fashionable, impossible, responsible, questionable, valuable, unthinkable, horrible, changeable, divisible, likeable (b) *Children will come up with their own explanations. Here is one possible one:* From the evidence, -ible would go after word parts ending in **s** or **r** or with double consonants. From the evidence, -able would go after word parts that end in a vowel or end in **n**.

2 impossible, unnecessary, illegal, insecure, irregular, inadequate, illogical, improper, unbelievable, inconvenient

3 beautiful, graceful, joyful, wonderful, bountiful

4 electrician, tension, completion, magician, confession, confusion, reflection, permission, possession

5 *This spelling test can be given more than once to check that your child has remembered the various spelling rules.*

Multiple-choice questions — Week 8 Monday

1 (a) his father may have been a sailor. (b) just before Christmas. (c) a building. (d) on his own.

2 (a) confused and frightened. (b) Edmund is human. (c) on a sledge.

3 (a) nothing. (b) she hadn't sold any matches. (c) in the evening.

Ordering and matching — Week 8 Tuesday

1 1 At first the mothballs will sink. 4 The mothballs lift to the surface again. 3 Bubbles of gas collect on the mothballs. 6 The mothballs sink to the bottom again. 2 The mothballs dance upwards. 5 At the surface, the gas escapes.

2 monkeys – boo, cows – bong, mice – clang, teapots – jibber jabber joo, trees – ping

3 Piccadilly Theatre – musical revue – evening; Cordoba Lounge – dance band – evening; Library/Card Room – bridge tournament – afternoon; Capri Bar – nightcap – late night

Finding words and phrases — Week 8 Wednesday

1 (a) She meant to ask Edmund if he was human, because Adam was the first man in the Bible. (b) dominions (c) *Choose from:* Edmund stood still, saying nothing; he was too confused; he seemed unable to move; he gave himself up for lost.

2 (a) *Choose from:* moonlit door; the quiet of the moonlight; faint moonbeams; dark stair; cropping the dark turf (b) perplexed (c) alliteration (d) smote

Expressing an opinion — Week 8 Thursday

1 (a) *The answer needs to include an opinion which is backed-up by facts from the text. Opinions supported by a simple statement, e.g. I liked reading the Little Match Girl because I felt sorry for her being cold, would not gain maximum marks.* (b) *Look for a logical interpretation of the story which shows understanding of the text. Avoid simple statements, e.g. I think she would have gone home.*

2 (a) *Look for an answer which gives either a lot of reasons why the rainforests should be saved, or explores one or two reasons thoroughly. Simple statements should be avoided in this type of question.* (b) *Allow either yes or no. The answer must also be supported by reasons from the text. No marks would be awarded for only circling yes or no.*

Comparing and contrasting texts — Week 8 Friday

1 (a) *Look for a detailed and well-thought out answer, along the lines of:* The letter from the Editor of the Langfield Echo is more objective as it deals with the facts in a less angry way than Mrs. Barrass' letter. Mrs. Barrass is angry because the cars are parking outside her children's school and she is worried because her children might get hurt, so she can't write objectively about it. The Editor of the Echo is interested but just writes about the facts of the case, without using angry words, because he is writing for all the readers of the Echo. (b) *Accept your child's choice of letter as long as it is backed up by facts.* For instance, some children may think Mrs. Barrass' letter is more effective, because she uses persuasive language to make you worried about the children getting knocked over. Other children may think the Editor's letter is more effective because it reaches more people and it is reporting on what the council is doing.

2 (a) *Accept your child's choice of articles as long as the opinion is backed up by reasons. Reasons for choosing the first report might be: it was more exciting; it was easier to read; you felt as if you were there. Reasons for liking the second article might be: it was clear; I liked the difficult words (some children do!) I enjoyed the description of the action; it gave you more background information.* (b) *Again accept your child's choice as long as it is backed up with reason. Most children will go for the first account as it is more exciting through its use of emotional language.*

Answers for Practice Reading Test

Cookie Snatchers

1 in the afternoon
2 lived in the house
3 in an office in her house
4 she was paying the milkman
5 she liked everything clean and tidy
6 She didn't want the children to eat any more cookies, so she put the jar up high out of their reach.
7 *Choose from:* there were no footprints in the soil; no cracked twigs or branches; no sign of a forced entry.
8 *Choose from:* crumbs on the floor; a kitchen chair slightly out of place; a spatula left on the draining board; a tightly scrunched up tea towel.
9 hampered means – got in the way of; slowed down; made things more difficult 10 *The answer must be backed-up with reasons and possibly references to parts of the text. Award 3 marks for a detailed answer; 3 marks for a less-detailed answer and 1 mark for a simple statement, e.g. I enjoyed the story because I like reading detective stories. No marks are awarded for choosing yes or no.*

Famous Literary Detectives and their Authors

11
Sherlock Holmes — Dr. Watson — Sir Arthur Conan Doyle
Hercule Poirot — Hastings — Agatha Christie
Lord Peter Wimsey — Bunter — Dorothy L. Sayers
Inspector Morse — Lewis — Colin Dexter
Lord Peter Wimsey — Harriet Vane — Dorothy L. Sayers

12 *Something similar to:* I think it is set out in boxes to make it easier to read and to find the information that you want; the boxes separate the different detectives and their authors so you can see who wrote about the different detectives; it keeps the same kind of information together.
13 *Something similar to:* The names of the authors are in bold as they are titles (subtitles) and are important information; they tell you what each box is going to be about.
14 A wine salesman who solved mysteries.
15 He got his name form the surnames of two cricketers: Sherlock and Holmes.
16 Colin Dexter
17 *Award 4 marks for four correctly matching pieces of information i.e. Two detectives and two authors; award 3 marks for three correct pieces.*
18 'Little grey cells' means he used his brain to solve crimes. He had to think hard and logically. 19 She disappeared for 11 days in 1926 and nobody knows where she went. 20 She was an elderly lady who dressed in tweed and a hat and she lived in a little village called St. Mary Mead. She looked like everyone's idea of a favourite granny.

Becoming a Reading Detective

21 an interview
22 She means reading carefully and putting together all the information you can in order to get the most out of a text.
23 *Accept answers along the lines of:* you look for clues in pictures; you look up words or ask other people like a detective asks other experts; you make notes to use later like a detective does in a notebook.
24 (i) national – all over a country; countrywide; you can read it anywhere in the country (ii) variety – selection, assortment, lots of different things (iii) inspire – make people want to do something; give people encouragement; make people want to do what you do.
25 She thinks this because we need reading for lots of things in everyday life like road signs, text messages, shopping lists etc. She thinks you should read a variety of material, so that the more you read, the more unusual words you will read and come to understand them.
26 *Award 3 marks for a detailed answer which expresses a preference and refers to the text. Award 2 marks for a less-detailed answer and 1 mark for a simple statement e.g. I liked the Cookie Snatchers because it was about a child being a detective, or I liked the interview because I want to be a reading detective.*